BUILDING

MINISTRY

TEAMS THAT

L. A. S. T.

PIETER VAN WAARDE

Building Ministry Teams That L.A.S.T., Copyright 2000

Published by AIS (Academic Information Systems)

5609 St. Charles Rd., Columbia, Missouri, 65202

ISBN # 0-9663422-4-0

C ONTENTS

P REFACE

I think you might have a love/hate relationship with this book.

On the one hand, it is likely that you will identify with many of the principles discussed here. You may even discover that you have tried them before. On the other hand, you may recall that the implementation of these concepts was anything but smooth. It is not that the ideas are complicated, for they are relatively simple in nature. It is the knowledge that when real life comes crashing through, team relationships often become one of the first casualties.

Even in the midst of writing this material, I found myself confronted by the need to apply one or more of these practices. Though I don't like to admit this, I did not want to do what was needed. I thought it would take too much time, too much energy and it often felt too risky. It seemed easier to pull a power move, or tell people to leave their feelings at home. I was often tempted to toss the idea of nurturing the team and instead, use whatever means necessary to get the job done.

These experiences reminded me again that building a team that will last requires a lot of effort, sometimes more effort than we are ready to give. When we think it's time to produce, someone else will want to address the process. At the moment we need to close a discussion, someone else will want to add one more point. Just at the time when we think we have dealt with our own stuff, the Lord will peel back one more layer. It is not always fun.

There *is* good news! It is worth it! The joy and fruitfulness of doing ministry as a team is worth the pain. There are few things that compare to the sense of partnership and joy that is experienced when synergy occurs and goals are reached. There is little else in this world that will bring such a sense of wonder, awe and God-honoring pride as when we can look at our fellow team members and say, "Look what we were able to accomplish together!"

It will be that vision and that hope, which will see us through the dry times. It will see us through the moments when we have to plow through hard conversations and make difficult decisions. It is that hope which will lift us up after a failure, and give us the strength to try again. It is that vision which merits our most earnest prayers and our most diligent efforts.

So as you begin, ask God for a picture of what this might look like for you and your team. Ask God to give you a sense of how good this can be. Then let that vision be the source of inspiration, for both yourself and your team! Because the truth is, you will need every bit of that inspiration. Teams that **L.A.S.T.** require a willingness to engage in a process that includes practices that are easy to define but difficult to apply:

> **L** osing Regularly
>
> **A** cknowledging Problems Early
>
> **S** haring Feelings Appropriately
>
> **T** aking Both Sides

Therefore, may He give you not only the vision to see its potential goodness, but the strength to give yourself diligently to its inevitable work!

A CKNOWLEDGMENTS

This book would not have been possible without the help and encouragement of many important people:

- my Lord and Savior Jesus Christ whose grace not only gave me a second chance, but whose guidance and strength continues to make team ministry a true joy every day

- my parents who always believed that I could and should do something like this

- my wife, whose loving support and honest feedback I cherished most of all

- my executive pastor Rod Casey who gave me the vocabulary for many of these concepts, and whose partnership has meant more than I can describe

- my editor Elsa Kok Cinjee whose input brought consistency and punch to the text, and who just so happens to be the best sister I could have ever hoped for

- my assistant Kim Nielsen who kept the rest of my life in order while the manuscript was being completed, and whose prayers always make a difference

- my staff at Woodcrest who helped me see and believe that doing ministry as a team could be more than just a nice idea

- my long-distance mentors Bill Hybels and John Maxwell,

whose example and teaching has literally changed the course of my life

- my good friends Casey and Shari Childers whose encouragement and gentle prodding caused me to finish the project in this lifetime

- my serendipitous lunch with Tim Elmore that moved me forward at a time when I felt stuck

- my board at Woodcrest who showed me that teamwork is not just a "staff thing"

- my publishers who shared the risk and took the plunge with me

- my friends and cheerleaders, many of whom the Lord used along the way with just the right word or just the right action at just the right time to keep me going—Chris and Lori, David and Casey, Beth and Wendy, Denise, Alan and Susan, Bradley, Eric and Jennifer, Jody, Rob and Grady, Todd, Rob and my co-laborers at Shoreline, Rick, Tom and Rebecca, Ralph and Diana, Bruce and Annie, Al and Cathleen, Teresa and Dana, Shawna, Diane, Art and Robyn, Kurt and Marsha, Barry and Tamra, Hu and Mary, and Nancy.

To my most important ministry team,
my family—
Carol, Pieter, Mallory and Curran

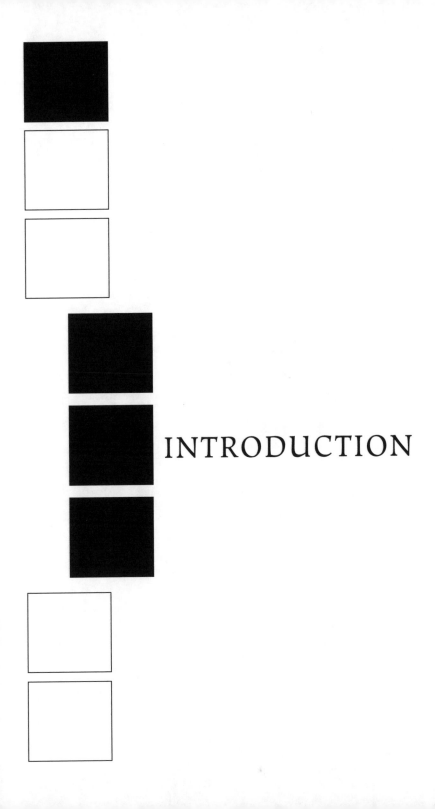

INTRODUCTION

T hroughout the 1980's, the rage in Business School was the study of entrepreneurs. They were considered the new pioneers in business, the engines that drove the economy. Yet at the same time, we were told that entrepreneurs were often too independent. We were told that they were reluctant to build effective partnerships that would ensure their long-term success. For that reason, we spent an enormous amount of time talking about the importance and benefits of being effective team-builders. In an ever-increasing competitive world economy, our survival as business leaders and entrepreneurs depended on it.

Strong teams were touted as the cure-all for staying ahead of the competition, retaining high quality staff members and maximizing return on investment. Our professors made a very compelling case! When I moved into a ministry context, teamwork was again promoted as "the way" to do ministry in this new generation. Comparisons were made to Paul's teaching on "body life" where every member knew their gifts and took their place. Books and conferences were developed to help pastors and leaders move to the new paradigm. The excitement of the movement and the promises made by the enthusiastic speakers, captured my heart. I wanted to experience the synergy of highly functioning teams. With these grand ideas and hopes in mind, I set out to build my own effective ministry team.

Typically, there is a fairly significant gap between the ideals we have in mind, and the reality of everyday ministry. That was my experience too. I realized that it was one thing to be philosophically convinced of the value of teamwork, but a very different thing to overcome the challenges of making teams work. The more involved I became with the day-to-day responsibilities of church life, the more difficult it became to actually experience the promised joys of team synergy and productivity. As a result, I read more profusely, attended additional conferences, and all the while remained convinced that this was the way I wanted to do ministry.

It seemed to me that this approach was not only Biblically responsible, but it fit my basic personality type. Because of this, I assumed that team building would come naturally. It didn't! I became increasingly frustrated by the lack of results. I wanted to be part of an effective ministry team, and hoped to eventually lead such a team. Yet every time I came back from the latest conference on "Team-based Ministry" there was a canyon-sized difference between what the conference leaders talked about, and what I was experiencing in my own team meetings.

My first inclination was to blame myself—maybe I wasn't cut out for this kind of work, maybe I wasn't even as committed as I should have been. After literally years of personal introspection and evaluation I realized that somewhere along the way I had missed something very important. That missing piece led to the writing of this book.

What did I miss? Teams *must* operate differently from the ground up. Philosophically, I was very much committed to the concept of teams. I was also quite hopeful about the promised benefits. Yet there were some behavioral practices that I needed to understand and apply in order to move from conceptual thinking to actual experience. Having had a chance to talk to others in similar situations, I discovered that it was the lack of these *behavioral adjustments* that also kept them from experiencing great teams.

In retrospect, I had a pretty naive perspective. I operated on the belief that if I was personally committed to the concept of teams and if I prayed long enough to experience the benefits, God would honor my intentions. I didn't give much thought to how I behaved or acted with the people on my team. I assumed that if we just put the right people in the same room, each of whom were equally committed toward this noble end, teamwork would just "happen."

That was the core problem with my approach.

INITIAL UNDERSTANDING

Philosophic Understanding

+

Strong Personal Commitment

+

the Right People

=

Highly Functioning Teams

Philosophic camaraderie and tenacious commitment alone (however well-intended) will not produce effective teams. Every person on the team must adopt certain practices that are conducive to team development, and those behavioral principles are the foundation for what follows.

If I were to illustrate the critical transition that I had to make, it would look like this:

PRESENT PRACTICE

Philosophic Understanding

+

Strong Personal Commitment

+

the Right People

+

Missing Component → Team-Building Practices

=

Highly Functioning Teams

We made that change. Woodcrest Chapel was the perfect environment for me to work these things out. As an innovative church, they seemed ready to try new ideas, not just in terms of the Sunday morning services, but throughout the week. Our greatest experiment however, was to try and do ministry as a team. It worked! It worked better than I imagined, but not without some heartache along the way. Even so, the lessons we learned about team development can be of value for others as well. It is joy to be able to pass these lessons on. May those who are so inclined (and committed) to practice what is described in these pages, experience the joy and fruitfulness that we have experienced (hopefully, without the heartaches!).

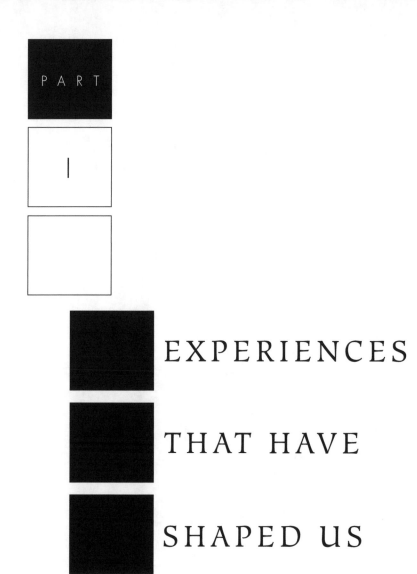

PART

I

EXPERIENCES

THAT HAVE

SHAPED US

THE JOY OF A GREAT TEAM

It was the end of another difficult season of ministry. I was reviewing the hardships in my mind:

- A popular staff member had recently resigned, and people were wondering what "really" happened.

- A fund-raising drive we completed brought in less money than anticipated, and I was imagining how that would affect budget planning and staff morale.

- A trusted board member was transferred out-of-state to take a new job, and there weren't any replacements readily apparent.

- Another core family had just decided to go to the church across town that "truly" taught the Bible.

The following day was Sunday—and that was the good news. Sundays were always the highlight of the week for me. It was when our team seemed most effective. I won't soon forget that particular day. I arrived early for rehearsal. A group of volunteers who served in the technical areas had already been setting up for half an hour. The music team had also arrived early and they were tuning their instruments. The drama team was rehearsing their lines one last time, and the smell of fresh coffee filled the air.

Our service director called us all together and walked us through the queue sheet. She made careful note of the transitions.

When she finished, we did every part of the service just as if it were the real thing. The music sounded great that day. After the praise set, Rod (our Executive Pastor) brought focus to the theme of the morning and set up the drama. The volunteer actors and actresses played their parts perfectly, and the folks setting up the chairs in the auditorium stopped for a moment to laugh at the antics of those in the sketch. They laughed because they saw themselves in the people on stage.

As I watched, I gained a fresh sense of excitement for what would take place in the services that morning. The drama nailed the questions that I would address in the message that followed. Once the drama rehearsal was complete, I reviewed the computer graphics that had the quotes and passages I would be using in the message. All was perfect. I gave the last line of the message, and the band returned for a final song. The soloist's words and voice were strong. When she finished, I was wiping away tears. I couldn't imagine anyone leaving that day unchanged.

We met in a small room before the service for prayer, one of the background singers had a special request for a friend who was coming to church for the first time in five years. She admonished me not to mess it up. We laughed and then prayed. I knew it was going to be a good day.

Five hours later, several of us were sitting on the front of the platform. Most of the people had left. It *was* a good morning. The church had been full for three services, but more importantly there was an obvious sense that God had graced us again with a work of His Spirit. People had been touched, the friend of the singer had come, and was quite impressed—she said we'd given her a lot to think about and that she would be back. That morning over 125 volunteers had served and given selflessly to pull off the services.

Later, we spent time reflecting on how good it was to be doing it together—each of us doing our part. There was nothing quite

like the feeling of a team of people sharing in the joys of being
used by God, where every person really appreciated the contri-
bution of the others. It was as though we were living the Biblical
truths that Jesus described. Even with the hardships, the disappointments and the things we had yet to figure out, we did know
one thing: *we couldn't imagine doing it any other way.*

Perhaps you have had those moments when it felt that good,
when everything was clicking on all eight cylinders. At times like
that—when you catch a small glimpse of how it is supposed to
be—a renewed sense of hope arises in your soul. It is those
moments that become the motivators to keep at it and hold you
steady when it isn't so great—when bickering, pettiness and self-
centeredness seem to rule the day.

HARD LESSONS AT THE START

When I first came to Woodcrest, my closest friends were cautiously
optimistic. It was a solid growing church, with strong dedicated
leaders. However, I was following the founding pastor, who had
"burned out" and left the church hastily. Trust was low, but expectations were high. The church was used to having a strong charismatic leader, and the congregation was used to doing ministry differently. Defining what "different" meant was no easy task, but my
wife and I were highly motivated, and we wanted to give it our all.

I have always been fairly relational in my approach to ministry,
so we quickly gained friends and allies in the new community. Much
to our surprise the church also continued to grow despite questions
surrounding the previous pastor's departure. It was the perfect environment to explore my hopes and dreams for team-based ministry.

Within six months we had added several new staff and launched
a building program. Soon it became apparent that my ideals for
building a strong team would take something more than just good

intentions. It would require that each member adopt new practices and behaviors in order to develop a highly functioning team.

I realized then that all my models for leadership (both in secular and Christian circles), had been based on a hierarchical approach, where the boss set the agenda, and the subordinates carried it out. As it turned out, that was not only *my* experience, it was the experience of everyone on our staff as well. Our concept of teamwork was that when the boss ran out of ideas, he/she would ask the group members for their suggestions. We didn't realize how those experiences had affected us. We just assumed that because we wanted to behave like a team, that teamwork would just naturally occur.

Looking back on it, I'm not sure I even realized what was happening. My thought was—we are all good people, we like each other, we are committed to doing this as a team, so it shouldn't take long for us to figure out how this should work. I was sadly mistaken. Teams are more than well-intentioned people sitting in the same room wanting to function as a team. It took us a while to come to that realization and unfortunately we experienced a few casualties along the way.

At times like that — when you catch a small glimpse of how it is supposed to be — a renewed sense of hope arises in your soul.

For each of us, our previous experiences had put us in a place where we subconsciously structured ourselves, and behaved in ways that actually circumvented the very process we were trying to create. It took us several years to discover that, and those were painful lessons. Although I remain convinced that the hardships were a necessary part of the learning curve, and in them God worked *His good* for all of us.

And we know that in all things God works for the good of those who love him and who have been called according to his purpose.

Romans 8:28

DEFINING TEAMWORK

+ What is a team?

+ How is a team different from a committee or a work group?

+ What is the role of team leader?

+ How do team members participate?

+ How are decisions made?

+ How do you deal with conflict?

These are important questions.

We discovered early on that these issues needed to be talked about regularly and agreed upon by every team member. In addition, certain standards had to be implemented that stretched across the entire organization in order for the process to remain consistent. Every time a new team member was added, these ideals had to be reviewed and re-engaged. This was important, because misunderstandings occur often and team dynamics are circumvented when people *assume* that everyone is on the same page.

. . . previous experiences had put us in a place where we subconsciously structured ourselves, and behaved in ways that actually circumvented the very process we were trying to create.

The subject matter of this book will discuss the details of how we have addressed these issues. In short, we employed a simple strategy: *articulate a few basic principles and make sure everyone understands them.* We talked about them often. They became our non-negotiables. We were also extremely proactive about our leadership development process. We invested heavily on the front end, and then gave team leaders fairly significant latitude in the implementation of the principles. We believed strongly in the adage, "stay clear on the main things and give liberty in the rest."

Before we discuss the particulars of our implementation, let me qualify the message we have to share.

NECESSARY PREREQUISITES

It is not my intent to suggest that this is the only—or even the best—way to do ministry. I believe there is a reason that the scriptures are vague about ministry structures. While the scriptures are very clear on ministry objectives, there is a deafening silence on structure and style. I believe that the reason for the silence stems from the Lord's delight in our staying dependent on His leadership. As a result, there are any number of ways that effective ministry can be carried out.

However, if a group determines to adopt a team approach, there are several prerequisites that are essential:

1. **SENIOR LEADERSHIP SUPPORT** It was our experience that initiating a team approach required wholehearted support of senior leadership. The amount of energy involved in implementing this methodology cannot be underestimated. Senior leadership's full commitment and endorsement was and is *always* essential.

2. **A RISK-TAKING SPIRIT** Unfortunately, as we endeavored to adopt this style, we discovered that there were not many working models to learn from. There were lots of people talking about doing team-based ministry, but there weren't many people actually *doing* it—at least that we could find. Therefore, effectiveness hinged on figuring out what teams needed to look like in our own setting with the group of people God had entrusted to us. That involved a lot of experimenting, and a general willingness to try a host of things in order to discover what worked.

3. **PERSEVERANCE** Repeated failure was common in the implementation phase. We can't underestimate the power of peoples' past experiences. What can make this even more challenging is that so many people are *talking* about teams these days that incoming staff and new volunteers typically respond with skepticism to team-building idealism. They have probably been in other places where teamwork vocabulary was common, *but* the practices were rarely consistent with the promises. Be prepared for team members to have their guard up. When we start talking about teamwork many will probably take a *wait and see* approach. The assignment during the transition is for leaders to continue communicating, instructing and most importantly, modeling what is expected.

Now, on to the practices!

LOSING

REGULARLY

Dealing with what happened inside of me was one of the hardest and most surprising elements of moving to a team-based ministry approach. I realized that if I wanted to build an effective team I had to be willing to set aside my desires, on both a personal and organizational level. The irony was that the more successful our team became the more I had to acquiesce to other team members. This is true universally. Every member of every team, and especially the leader, must "lose" regularly.

For example, as Senior Pastor of a growing church, I initially had influence in almost every area. I preached all the messages, I led all the staff meetings, I conducted all the weddings and counseled all those who needed emotional support. I had input on the selection of every leader, I baptized all the new converts, and occasionally played in the band. I complained about the fact that I didn't have the chance to focus on anything in particular, but I also received all the accolades.

When we started adding staff and capable volunteers, I had to be willing to let go of those areas where others had greater expertise. At first that was easy, and I was more than willing to hand over most of those responsibilities. Yet with the delegation of responsibility, I also needed to be willing to grant authority for the relevant decision-making. The new leaders didn't always choose to do things in the way I would have done them. In addition, they began to receive some of the praise that I used to receive. I'd like to say I was big enough to be okay with that, but there were times when that was more difficult than I cared to admit.

Over time, I began to resent the loss of influence. I became concerned about how people saw me, and whether or not I was still considered a valued and vital member of the team. I also had difficulty knowing where to retain oversight and when to just let things go—especially if it meant a loss of impact, productivity, and/or quality.

I remember when this really hit home for me. It seemed like a small thing, but it is illustrative of the lesson I had to learn. Early on, I was involved with developing the programming elements of our services (music, drama, video clips, etc.). Because those elements require significant advance preparations, I would go on a regular quarterly study break, and spend several days in prayer and fasting. In the process, I would develop various themes, which we would address in our Sunday morning services. I would also bring back suggestions for music selections and drama vignettes, ideas I thought would appropriately enhance or introduce the Sunday morning message.

Once we hired our music minister, I discovered he wanted to have some input on these elements as well. Being the secure budding team-building leader that I was, I delegated that responsibility to him. I told him I would continue making my suggestions, but if he had a better idea he could feel free to insert it. Well, it wasn't long before I discovered fewer of my ideas were making the cut. More often than not, it was his ideas that were finding their way on to the programming list. To his credit, his elements and ideas were usually more effective.

But I didn't really like it.

I had to make a critical decision at that point. I had to decide if it was more important that my idea be used, or that this new staff member have an opportunity to develop in his role as a valued member of the team. I could have insisted that my ideas be used. I could have even spiritualized it and told him I had heard from God about these things—I had prayed and fasted about these ideas. Had he been equally as devout?

Our music minister had the character and integrity such that he would have submitted to my leadership, and done it *my* way. If I had insisted on that however, I wouldn't have had the active and engaged *team* member that he became. We wouldn't have experienced the dynamic services that changed lives in the way they did as a result of his participation. I would have circumvented the development of the team, and reduced the impact of the ministry.

It sounds so cut and dry on paper—doesn't it? But at the moment when those thoughts were raging in my mind, it was anything but easy. It felt risky. I felt insecure, and it was hard to know what to do with the emotions. This much was for sure—I was beginning to learn a lesson. If I was serious about team building, it would require a willingness to lose regularly. There was hardly a day that went by where I didn't have to remind myself of that time and again.

The new leaders didn't always choose to do things in the way I would have done them. In addition, they began to receive some of the praise that I used to receive. . . . Over time, I began to resent the loss of influence.

It was not unlike what John the Baptist experienced with the arrival of Jesus. For a season John was the center of attention. People were coming to him, he was receiving all the focus, and God was using him to prepare the way for the Lord. However, at the appointed time, Jesus moved to the forefront and John had the maturity to understand the need to defer to the Master.

He must become greater; I must become less.

John 3:30

As much as we may have known that this was the necessary way of ministry, that didn't make it any easier to walk through the hardship of it all.

KNOWING YOUR ROLE

In order to survive the pain of losing, team members have to be secure in their role. All too often our security is tied to our position and/or our job responsibilities. We connect our value to the organization, and sometimes even to God in terms of what we do, instead of who we are. It is so easy for that phrase to become a platitude—*your value is tied to who you are, not what you do*. We throw it around to sound spiritually astute, but the ramifications are indeed significant.

The truth is, we have been specifically designed for a God-given life role. This role, once defined, can be played out within any organization. If we are secure in our roles, we are much more willing to let go of the tasks that once defined us.

For example, if I had interpreted my value to the church as being *the* person who selected programming elements for every service, then I would have been unwilling to let go of that task. If God had designed my role to be *about* programming, then yes, I would have had a responsibility to stick with it and do it well. However, if it was not part of my God-given role (and I held on to it out of personal insecurity), then I would have been sinning twice. Once, because I was thwarting what God wanted to do through me, and twice, because I was keeping someone else from fulfilling his or her God-given role.

Defining our God-given role is not an easy task. In the day-to-day responsibilities of church life some of what we do is more *seasonal* in nature and relates to a specific need/time in the ministry. Other parts of what we do are *core* and relate to our calling and over-arching life assignment. Time and experience help us to discern between these two dimensions of what we do (that which is needful for a season) and who we are (fulfilling our unique God-given role). Yet, in the end, it is only God that can give us ultimate clarity. For that reason, our staff became enthusiastic advocates of using personal retreats to discover and define our roles.

His divine power has given us everything we need for life and godliness through our knowledge of him who called us by his own glory and goodness . . . . Therefore, my brothers, be all the more eager to make your calling and election sure.

II Peter 1:3 & 10

Early in my ministry, I learned the value of taking time away for planning and message preparation. I was a person who was easily distracted by the daily duties of ministry life. Eventually it just became a matter of professional necessity for me to withdraw in order to plan and prepare well. I had been doing that for 15 years. But since then, the value of retreats expanded beyond planning purposes. They became an essential time (for myself and many of our team members) to discern our God-given roles.

These personal retreats were typically 2–3 days out of town (several retreats might be required if someone is at the front end of the discovery process). The agenda for the retreat revolved around asking several questions:

- What am I spending most of my time doing?

- Is it consistent with what I know of my spiritual gifts, ministry passion, personal make-up, and ministerial calling?

- What adjustments can I make in my weekly routine/job responsibilities in order to work in a way that corresponds with what I know of who I am?

NOTE: For a more detailed description of how to plan a personal retreat refer to Appendix 1.

In our organization, when a team member returned from a personal retreat, they would meet with their team leader to negotiate possible adjustments in ministry responsibilities (if applicable). This became important in order to ensure that at least 75–80% of their job duties would be consistent with what they understood about their ministry role.

Let me give an example of what this looks like on paper.

I was called by Woodcrest to serve as the Senior Pastor. That was my job title, but it took me five years to define that role. My role, as I learned to define it, involved four things: teaching, leading, inspiring and relating. Those were things that I knew were transferable to any environment. Once I was clear on the core contributions in consultation with the Board of Directors, I worked them into the context of my job responsibilities at Woodcrest.

Senior Pastor

1. Teaching (50%)

   - Plan and preach 42 Sundays each year.
   - Plan and teach in 20 Community Live services each year (mid-week service, held twice/month).
   - Lead and teach a bi-weekly small group Bible Study that meets in my home.
   - Help plan and teach at leadership functions:
     — Leadership Summit: annual leadership event
     — Leadership Woodcrest: quarterly class
     — Leadership Hour: monthly luncheon

◆ Outside speaking and consulting (6–8 engagements each year)

2. Leading (25%)

   ◆ Chairman of the Board of Directors

   ◆ Point person for Leadership Team (senior staff)

3. Inspiring (15%)

   This was a fairly nebulous (but critical) part of the role, which involved being aware of people and places within the church that might need my personal attention. It included encouraging, supporting, exhorting, and casting vision. This usually happened quite informally, perhaps I would take someone to lunch. I would make time to walk slowly through the office to check-in and chat with staff and volunteers. I would also make myself available after services to counsel and pray with people and/or send encouraging notes and e-mails.

4. Relating (10%)

   This is what I did to relate to people outside our local church:

   ◆ Chamber of Commerce

   ◆ Denominational meetings

   ◆ Community-wide pastor fellowships

   ◆ Personal evangelism

NOTE: Other examples of these kinds of role descriptions can be found in Appendix 2.

The salient point for me was that my job description correlated with the role that I knew was God-ordained. It fit who I was, and it was consistent with what I knew I had to do, regardless of my job title. I was extremely clear about what I had to accomplish, and I didn't have to obsess over what I couldn't do. I also didn't feel as frustrated when I had to lose—which as already stated—happened quite regularly.

The other practical benefit was that I didn't have to spend much time trying to figure out what my week looked like. I didn't have to wonder about other people's expectations. It didn't really matter what my position or title was, because the role was what I *had to* do in order to be faithful to God and myself. If the church decided that the Senior Pastor at Woodcrest needed to fulfill different duties, I believe I would have been able to release the position, because my value was not connected to my title. That was tremendously liberating!

Almost everyone on our team went through a similar kind of role definition process. Each person who worked through it, found the experience equally beneficial. It kept each of us from becoming territorial. It allowed people to make transitions within the organization with minimal emotional stress. It created tremendous personal ownership of the ministry. People were doing what they loved to do and what they felt called to do. I had to spend very little time checking up on people, because there was a high-degree of personal motivation and accountability. As a result, "losing" became less painful for all of us.

That is not to say that it was painless.

THE "LAS VEGAS PRINCIPLE"

I can imagine the head shaking that is going on for those who may have just finished reading the last section. It can't be that easy! After all . . .

- There are always things that need to be done that are unpopular and/or inconvenient.

- Nobody loves everything about his or her job.

- What happens when there is a difference between what a team member loves to do, and what the team leader thinks should be done?

These are valid concerns, and we certainly had our share of tension-filled negotiations.

Before you toss the book, let me elaborate.

First, we conceded that at best we would love 75–80% of what we do—a good percentage in any situation. Therefore, 20-25% of our work would not be the most enjoyable, but was still necessary. In short, we realized that there were some things that we would have to accept as part of our responsibility to the organization. In fact, in some cases when people first joined the ministry, those percentages were probably more like 50/50. Yet even in those early days, the so-called distasteful parts of our job became great opportunities for personal growth. Discovering what we don't like, or becoming aware of things for which we are ill-suited, can be just as important as discovering what we love.

Second, it is critical for team leaders and team members to engage in meaningful negotiations. This was where we came up with the *Las Vegas Principle*. While we did not condone gambling there were certain parallels worth noting. When someone goes to Vegas, and they decide to participate at the gaming tables, they typically determine beforehand how much they can afford to lose. They will treat a $5 bet different from a $100 bet, and they may never consider wagering $1,000,000.

In a similar way, we had certain issues/ideals (personal and corporate) that were about as valuable to us as a $5 bet. If we lost, it wouldn't really affect our lifestyle in a significant way. Then there were other issues that were more valuable, perhaps along the lines of $10,000 or maybe even $1,000,000. As we approached our discussions about ministry responsibilities and roles, we entered those negotiations with an assigned value to the various issues we wanted to discuss. We each determined beforehand the areas in which we were willing to "lose," and where we were non-negotiable. As a result, when we were discussing the points of contention we could be clear about the critical issues, and we didn't have to treat every point as a $1,000,000 cause.

We each determined beforehand the areas in which we were willing to "lose," and where we were non-negotiable.

For example, we had some members of our team that came out of tradition where infant baptism was an important part of their spiritual heritage. We were strong proponents of post-conversion immersion. It was probably a $500,000 issue for us (as a church). Preferences regarding mode of baptism would not affect a person's capacity to participate on the team, unless infant-baptism was a $1,000,000 issue for them. Only then would it become a point of serious contention, the outcome of which could affect their role on the team.

There are always issues like this in every church: end-time theology, charismatic expression in public worship, the use of secular music in services, preferences regarding Bible translations, etc. Since our church appealed to people from a wide variety of backgrounds, it was important for us to have the vocabulary whereby we could have these kind of meaningful discussions. The *Las Vegas* principle gave us the freedom to talk about them without sacrificing relationships.

Now that we have broached the topic of negotiation, it would be wise to comment on the importance of conflict resolution.

EMBRACING THE CONFLICT

One of the real challenges facing those who want to develop highly functioning teams, is the recognition that many team members typically have a general unwillingness to engage in any kind of conflict. It is at this point where the Church's commitment to being "nice" really works against us. It seems that in all too many settings there is an unwritten rule that if two Christians have a heated exchange (especially professional ministers) this is seen as unloving and inappropriate. It is expected that we accept whatever comes our way and not get too emotional or express strong opinions—especially to our leaders. However, this rarely leads to effective teamwork, and more often than not encourages gossip, slander and bitterness.

Let me be clear, I am not suggesting that embracing conflict gives us license to be disrespectful, argumentative, or abusive. But it does mean that we have to learn how to accept the discomfort that comes from engaging each other.

The prospect of this kind of intensity really shouldn't surprise us, especially when we consider the gravity of what we are dealing with. In ministry we are given a sacred trust. We are charged with the responsibility of giving watch care over people's souls. Their eternal destiny is at stake. We have given our lives to perhaps the most important work there is. It is often gut wrenching work. Is it any wonder we feel so deeply about so many things?

We basically have this choice: process our emotions fully and appropriately . . . or go destructive.

Conflict was certainly an integral part of the landscape in the early church. Even though we are not given the details of the discussion of what took place at the Counsel of Jerusalem in Acts 15, even a cursory reading suggests that there was a long and heated debate about the importance and necessity of circumcising Gentile believers. By using even a small degree of our imagination we can envision the passion. The intensity of the emotion would have been obvious to everyone there.

In 1997, researchers with California Management Review measured the relationship between senior management's capacity for interpersonal conflict and their organization's responsiveness to market changes. The study, which observed 12 high-tech firms in the Silicon Valley, concluded that in those settings where conflict was embraced (and even encouraged), there was a significantly higher capacity to meet consumer needs. Stop and think about that for a moment.

More conflict = Better business

Doesn't that make sense? When people are willing to engage in healthy conflict several things happen:

+ Irrational assumptions are challenged.

+ Outdated ideas and practices are brought under scrutiny.

+ People's imaginations are engaged.

+ Problems are addressed in the open where they can be dealt with and not buried.

Whether we look in the scriptures or in the market place, we discover the reality and potential productivity of conflict. The challenge, of course, is learning to do this well. For many, that is a very intimidating prospect, but it is essential for effective team development.

Since effective conflict resolution is so critical, keep these basic principles in mind:

+ Conflict is inevitable, and needs to be embraced.

+ Conflict is understandable given what is at stake in ministry.

+ Refusing to embrace conflict is personally detrimental, and hinders team development.

♦ Embracing the conflict does not give us the right to be divisive or destructive.

♦ Effective conflict management leads to stronger teams, and greater fruitfulness in ministry.

At this point, you may feel a bit overwhelmed. Take heart, it will also *feel* overwhelming when you're in the midst of it! For that reason, it becomes vitally important to process through the emotions that we experience in the throes of healthy conflict resolution.

PROCESSING OUR EMOTIONS

I have dedicated an entire chapter to healthy emotional processing (in Part IV), but let me introduce you to some of the basics here.

One of the things that I have discovered about people who give themselves to full-time Christian service is that we are generally uncomfortable dealing with emotions—especially our own. Yet ministry, by its very nature, is quite emotional. Our tendency, however, is to discount the importance and power of our feelings. We usually work very hard at subordinating our emotional life to our spiritual convictions, which is certainly the ultimate goal for every area of life.

We are taught (and we teach) that everything we do must come under the lordship of Christ—appropriately so!

And he is the head of the body, the church; he is the firstborn from among the dead; so that in everything he might have the supremacy.

Colossians 1:18

Unfortunately, when it comes to our emotions, we often minimize them and attempt to overcome them by saying things like, "I shouldn't feel this way," or "This doesn't honor God." We endeavor, by sheer will-power, to speak and act "rightly." Certainly there is a time for this kind of intentional application of Biblical principles, as long as we don't circumvent the godly purpose of our emotions.

One of the most meaningful talks I ever heard on this subject was at a Willow Creek Pastor's Conference in 1990. Bill Hybels was talking about a difficult season in his own ministry, and he gave a message entitled "Gifts, Gauges and Games." In the talk, he shared about how he had essentially ignored the emotional needs in his life for years, and it nearly shipwrecked his life and ministry. It was only as he learned to monitor the "emotional gauge" that he began to find a sense of balance and wholeness.

That was the first time in my life that I had heard such a highly respected pastor speak so poignantly on the subject of emotional health—without over-simplifying or over-spiritualizing. The principles he talked about became foundational for me in my own battle to retain a sense of balance and emotional health.

As it related to dealing with the losses I have described thus far, it meant that I had to make time to grieve. I had to be honest about what I was feeling when I had to give things up. I needed to acknowledge the difficulties I had with the loss of influence, the loss of privacy, and the blown conflict-resolution sessions. I had to find safe places and safe people who could help me process. I had no qualms about seeking professional help when I felt stuck, and I did so on several occasions.

The challenge for many of us is to go "spiritual." We tend to want to give ourselves positive spiritual pep talks. We remind ourselves of the martyrs who suffered torture and were burned at the stake. We think of the missionaries who are laboring overseas, or the heroes of scripture who seemed to serve tirelessly. We feel guilty and immature because our feelings get hurt when someone fails to recognize our hard work, or when a staff member doesn't take one of our suggestions.

But truthfully, what are we going to do with these feelings—even if we count them as immature? To quote a Bible verse and essentially "stuff it" may work for the moment, but if that becomes the way we deal with all our emotional baggage it will most certainly come back to haunt us in the future.

An illustration we have often used is that of the "beach ball." If you have ever tried to hold a beach ball under water, you understand something about the difficulty of stuffing emotions. We can do it with one for a while, and perhaps even with two. Yet it is impossible to continue holding them in check as life happens. Ultimately, they will surge to surface, leaving us breathless and feeling out of control. So it is with our unresolved emotions.

The challenge for ministry-types is that we feel the need to be strong and unwavering. However, the reality we must face is that our emotions will find expression. If not through healthy processing, than through depression, burnout, addictions and/or unhealthy compulsions. We basically have this choice: process our emotions fully and appropriately . . . or go destructive.

Interestingly enough, I discovered that I was not the only one on staff who had to process emotions. Everyone on the team had their own emotional challenges, and as a team leader I had to give the rest of the team permission to do their own processing as well.

CHAPTER SYNOPSIS

At the outset, team-based ministry sounds so noble and grand. The promise of deep enduring relationships and becoming part of something better than anything we could ever do on our own, sounds very appealing. However, becoming a team and building a team is hard. Some of the hardest work is the work we have to do on the inside.

- ♦ We should prepare ourselves for regular losses ;
- ♦ Spend time defining our role so the losses won't defeat us;
- ♦ Know what the $1,000,000 issues are, and bet accordingly;
- ♦ Let us accept the reality of conflict and fight fair;
- ♦ Process what we're feeling, so that we won't be surprised by the surging "beach ball."

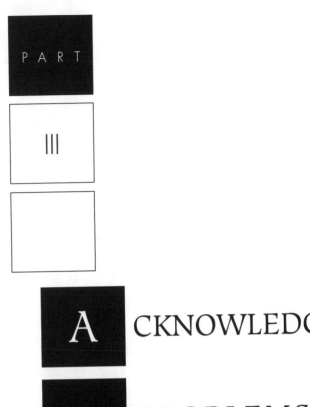

PART

III

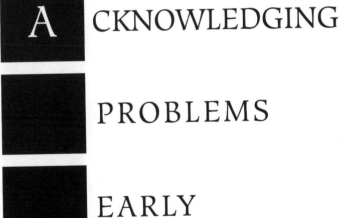

ACKNOWLEDGING

PROBLEMS

EARLY

C ollins and Porrus in their book *Built to Last,* made an interesting observation about innovative institutions. Before they wrote their book they assumed that visionary organizations would always be a great place to work. Yet what they discovered, was that people typically had a love / hate relationship with those companies. Some people absolutely loved working there, while others didn't ever really "fit," and ended up leaving. The key for those who stayed was their capacity to understand and embrace their particular organization's unique corporate culture.

The same is true when it comes to developing a team-based approach to church work. It takes a unique individual to become part of a church staff that is endeavoring to employ teams as the way they do ministry. People are rarely neutral in their response to this approach—they either love it and flourish, or they hate it and leave.

We discovered this the hard way. We had been in interviewing sessions with potential team members, and talked at length about *the way we played.* We would ask repeatedly, "Do you understand what we are saying? Are you ready to do the internal and interpersonal work necessary in order to function as part of a ministry team?" In the interview there was regularly an enthusiastic affirmation. But within several months it became clear that they didn't really understand and weren't ready to do the work.

Their response did not make them bad people or ineffective ministers. It just meant that they had to find a context and culture that was more consistent with their own personality and style. Those scenarios caused us to be even more intentional and up front in our communication when we described team ministry. In addition, we had to become increasingly cautious about giving away roles and responsibilities without first ensuring a thorough understanding of our organizational culture.

TAKING THE SLOW ROAD

One of the real attractive points of team-based ministry is the prospect of intimate relationships. When teams are functioning well, relational intimacy is a wonderful by-product. Not surprisingly, it is also the more relationally oriented people that are the ones typically drawn to a team approach. The temptation then, is to be immediately drawn to those with a kindred spirit and to connect relationally before we have a chance to test the organizational fit.

I discovered it was always easier to move forward relationally than it was to try to back up.

As a more relationally oriented person, I had to learn to force myself to be more measured in giving my heart away. Initially, I was quite resistant to the idea of having to restrict my natural inclinations. However, the school of hard knocks convinced me of the value of taking the slow road. I discovered it was always easier to move forward relationally than it was to try to back up. Therefore, taking reasonable relational steps (and keeping the pace more intentional) saved everyone the grief of having to try and back track. Again, this was one of those issues, which was easy to theorize about and difficult to practice.

On one occasion, I had a conversation with someone serving as my administrative assistant. She was someone I enjoyed working with and we were quite comfortable with each other on a relational level. She was also relatively new to the team, and we hadn't had the chance to engage in much conflict. So when we had a difference of opinion on how a certain situation should be handled, it created a real dilemma for her. She knew about our conviction to deal with problems early and in a straightforward fashion. However, she was concerned that if she shared her misgivings it might have an adverse affect on our working relationship.

To her credit, she was able to press past her ambivalence and talk openly about her concerns. Yet not without a sense of risk. This is the point at which many team members choose not to engage. It's a lot easier to decide not to risk, and to discount the importance of the event or the feelings associated with it. At first, it *is* always easier. However, our early choices quickly became ingrained practices, and if we can't engage on the "small stuff," we'll have greater difficulty engaging on the more significant matters.

For this reason, we endeavored to make a big deal out of the often-awkward early attempts by team members to take relational risks in speaking truth. Often they would fumble their way through it, and they usually didn't say everything in the way we might have hoped. Sometimes it even felt a little trivial. Yet it was these early experiences that were so important in shaping future behavior. It was especially critical for team leaders to understand the dynamics. There was tremendous future potential unleashed when a leader acknowledged and encouraged the early attempts at truth-telling. I can't over-state how important it is for leaders to give team members permission to *go there*.

It is equally important for team leaders to go there as well. Often leaders can be just as reluctant to engage in addressing areas of concern. Ministry is a volunteer intensive work, and good volunteers (and quality staff) are hard to find. Therefore, if we have found someone who is faithful or talented, it is very tempting to side-step the process of dealing with problem/concerns because we don't want to risk losing the team member. Be assured however, problems do not resolve themselves, and they do not go away. When problems remain unresolved, they usually intensify.

Make a personal note and pin it to the wall—*"There is no such thing as an irreplaceable team member."* It doesn't matter how gifted they are. It doesn't matter how much money they give. It doesn't matter how influential they are in the church or how loudly they can yell. They are not irreplaceable.

All too many ministry leaders have sacrificed the team process in order to retain a star player. Ultimately what is produced has little lasting fruit, and what little fruit that is produced is hardly worth the energy and effort it takes to put up with the destructive patterns of a non-team player.

This can be an especially difficult principle to live with when we consider how hard it might be to replace the star. Especially if we think our job might be at stake. So, let me list a few benefits of playing this way. We might want to tack this list on the wall as well:

+ Ministry is extremely energy-intensive. Consider the new creative resource base we would have if we didn't have to waste so much time accommodating someone else's unresolved issues.

+ If this person is as difficult with others as they are with us (and it is certainly quite likely that they are), we might be surprised by the fact that others will actually applaud our courage to deal with the situation.

+ If we're honest with ourselves, we will realize that we are probably taking out our frustrations on others who don't deserve it, most likely our family. Think of the added grace that we'll receive at home / church if these folks don't have to feel the brunt of our misdirected frustrations.

+ We will gain new respect and loyalty from other existing team members who will see first hand that we are individuals of principle, and that we can't be bought by money, talent or power.

♦ God may want to use our loving confrontation as a critical next step in this person's spiritual growth and maturity. Imagine what it might be like if he/she really could change, and God used us to help bring that about.

♦ If it costs us our job, we can at least leave with our integrity in place—no small thing in the grand scheme of life.

I can also say from personal experience, that every time I made one of these hard calls—and I did so with integrity and not out of spite or malice—the Lord always followed up that decision with an unexpected blessing of new resources and new people.

Remember, the earlier we address these issues the easier it is, and the longer we wait, the harder it becomes!

THE FINAL 10%

At one of the Church Leadership Conferences at Willow Creek, we heard Bill Hybels talk about the importance of speaking the last 10%.

It confirmed to us that people dealing with problems (especially early on) say about 80–90% of what they really want to say—then they stop. By saying that much, they did what was expected. The basic message was communicated. But they didn't go further. They typically would avoid the final 10%.

For example, if we were in the process of evaluating a Sunday morning service it was easy for the team members to focus their critiques on 90% of the service. Then there was that final 10% that was harder to talk about—the sexist comment made by the person giving the announcements, the awkward transition between the drama and the special music, or the fact that we started rehearsal 15 minutes late (again). These comments are typically easier left unsaid, until the frustrations run so high that team members either blow-up or quit. Therefore, we endeavored to give people permission, from the outset, to talk about the final 10%.

Why is it so hard?

+ Some of us are not used to confrontation, and the first 90% is hard enough.

+ Some of us are concerned that we will end up saying it wrong and be misunderstood.

+ Some of us are convinced that the relationship is not strong enough to bear that level of truth telling.

+ Some of us are worried that what we say will be held against us.

+ Some of us are afraid that we will be labeled disloyal, argumentative, or unkind.

+ Some of us are hesitant because we have our own issues, and feel hypocritical about offering any kind of critique.

Each of these concerns is valid in their own right, and shouldn't be summarily dismissed. However, let us consider the following perspectives:

"I hate conflict!" — If we are going to take the time and energy to engage in truth telling, and we don't say all that is really on our hearts to say, won't that simply mean more confrontation in the future? Therefore, it stands to reason that the more confrontation-adverse we are, the more proactive we should be to take full advantage of each opportunity.

"But, I'll be misunderstood!" — If we fear misunderstanding, and as a result choose not to share the final 10%, doesn't that actu-

ally increase the likelihood of being misunderstood? It is in the final 10% where the real *truth nuggets* lie. It is what contains the essence of what we really believe. If we want to be clear, and avoid misunderstanding, we have all the more motivation to work hard at sharing it.

"This feels so risky!" — Why must truth telling be perceived as having largely a negative impact on relationships? Is it not also possible that when hard truth is shared in an appropriate manner it can actually improve the quality of a relationship? Honest communication, that includes the final 10%, invariably builds trust and does not diminish it.

"I'll be rejected!" — Good information is essential for quality decision-making. No team member or organization concerned about growing learning and/or improving themselves rejects honest thoughtful feedback. If we are rejected for speaking truthfully, we are either in an unhealthy organization or we are dealing with an insecure team member.

"I'll be seen as a troublemaker!" — Negative labels are rarely bestowed on those who share the final 10% *appropriately.* Rather, those designations are reserved for those whose actions are incongruent with their speech, or for those who under the guise of being honest, resort to personal attacks and name-calling.

"I have my own stuff!" — The scriptures do admonish us to share with others circumspectly—always considering our own frailty and sinfulness. However, the Bible addresses the avoidance of speaking truthfully with equal weight. Often our unwillingness to do so is more often a sign of pride than of genuine humility.

When we first started talking about this principle with our staff, I was also working with a relatively new member of the team who had come out of a business background. She was quite uncomfortable with this idea of sharing the final 10%, because she had some bad experiences with that kind of truth-telling in her past. For this reason, she viewed the whole idea with a good bit of skepticism. However, after several weeks of working at the church she came to me with something that would qualify as the final 10%.

I had always taken real personal satisfaction in the fact that I operated as a *permission-giving* leader. I enjoyed letting people find their own way and work in a manner that was consistent with their own style. I had few rules, and essentially gave people the liberty to do their jobs in a way that seemed best to them. Many people on the team thrived under that kind of freedom. However, for the new team member, my leadership style was anything but freeing. It was actually quite frustrating because she had no idea of what I expected until an expectation wasn't met. After a few of these unpleasant experiences, she asked for a meeting with me, where she explained lovingly and honestly how she was feeling.

People dealing with problems say about 80–90% of what they really want to say. . . . Then there is that final 10% that is harder to talk about. . . .

She prefaced her comments by reiterating her appreciation for the ministry and for my leadership. Then she went on to say that she felt lost by the lack of specifics about her responsibilities. She sited some examples of how this had hurt her effectiveness, and thwarted the purposes of the ministry. It was a significant conversation for both of us, and as a result of her candor we were able to make some adjustments in the role, and in the communication she received. For the next few months we monitored the process, and over time she began to feel much more productive.

On the surface this may appear as a small thing. However, these kinds of conversations are rarely held. Usually, these frustrations are vented around the water cooler with fellow employees. Sometimes people work for years in a situation that is on the verge of intolerable—all because they are unwilling to address the final 10% with those who need to hear it.

In the situation I just cited there were benefits for both of us. I learned something about my leadership style. It became a growth opportunity for me. The team member felt heard and appreciated, accommodations were made so that she could be more productive. She was also spared the heartache of a growing resentment that would have eventually tainted her ministry and damaged her soul. All that would have been missed had she not been willing to share the final 10%.

Most of what has been addressed to this point is related to the harder 10%, and saying the things that we imagine might be difficult for others to hear. The same principles apply when it relates to encouragement and affirmation. Sometimes we are just as hesitant to build people up for the very same reasons we are hesitant to confront. Yet when we fail to do so, we also miss some wonderful opportunities to experience the benefits that make a team such a great thing to be a part of—namely the joy of doing things well!

THE IMPORTANCE OF QUALIFIERS

When I finished writing the last section on sharing the final 10%, it was at the end of a long day of laboring behind the computer screen. I felt good about the work I had done. When my wife came to review it, I was waiting for her glowing report on how meaningful and inspirational the section was. Instead, she reminded me of all the failed attempts when people on our team, or disgruntled church members, endeavored to share their heartfelt thoughts and it hardly worked as well as I just described.

Apparently, sharing the final 10% was not difficult for her.

Her comments were significant. They forced me to compare the times when the idea worked well and the times when it didn't work as well. Often the difference could be attributed to the approach, and/or the attitude of those who were sharing their concerns. The content of a message (regardless of its legitimacy) is often considered and engaged in light of the manner in which it's delivered.

If someone shares a concern with a condescending tone, or if they come to someone assuming they know all the facts, it puts the person receiving it on the defensive. It is amazing how just a few well-placed qualifiers can shape the outcome of a conversation. Typically, these are things we are already thinking, but we shouldn't underestimate the value of voicing them.

For example, prefacing a concern with a phrase like, *I may not know everything that has gone into this decision, but it appears to me . . .* or *Perhaps you have already given this a lot of thought, but it seems as though . . .* These kind of qualifying statements communicate our understanding that there is often more to any situation than what is readily apparent. They communicate a belief in the integrity and noble intentions of the other person. They communicate trust and appropriate self-awareness. The end result is typically much more positive—both in terms of the particular situation and the relationship.

> **Such qualifiers communicate a belief in the integrity and noble intentions of the other person. They communicate trust and appropriate self-awareness.**

Consider the difference when a critique is introduced by a statement like this, *I know you guys don't really care about this, but you should know that . . .* or *When you say/do that it makes me feel . . .* These kind of introductory remarks set up an adversarial tone from the outset. And the outcome is rarely positive.

I have heard it said that these kind of verbal gymnastics are a waste of time. The truth is words *are* important. They are powerful tools that shape the context of our conversational environment, and they significantly effect our capacity to relate to people. To the degree that we ignore their power, to that same degree we undermine relationships and ministry.

> *A bit in the mouth of a horse controls the whole horse. A small rudder on a huge ship in the hands of a skilled captain sets a course in the face of the strongest winds. A word out of your mouth may seem of no account, but it can accomplish nearly anything—or destroy it!*
>
> The Message, James 3: 3–5

THE MEANS MATTER

Equally significant to the words we use, is the manner in which we communicate them. In our day, there has been an explosion of new and better ways to communicate—fax machines, cell phones, e-mail etc.. There is no question that these new tools have made the process of sending and receiving information much easier. However, in order to honor the team members, it is important to be sensitive about the medium we use to share our different thoughts and concerns.

Because of the volume of information people deal with on a daily basis, we all make decisions (often subconsciously) about which pieces of information will receive priority attention. We tend to attach a certain value to the content of the message simply by virtue of the means by which it is communicated. Typically the more personalized the means, the more attention we will give to the content.

For example, if I asked to meet personally with a team member, whatever was said in that meeting was automatically of higher value than whatever I might have written later in an e-mail. The challenge for team members and leaders is to match the weight of the message with the appropriate communication vehicle. Problems arise when we mismatch the content and the tool.

Communication Tool	Subtle Message Communicated
Pre-arranged Personal Meeting (office)	Formal, Clear Agenda, Critical Info.
Pre-arranged Personal Meeting (lunch)	Less Formal, Agenda, Significant
Spontaneous Personal Meeting	Check-in, Relational, Important
Team Meetings	General, Planned, Big Picture
Phone Call (from office)	Short, Specific Information
Phone Call (from home)	Emergency? Immediate Action
Phone Call (from cell phone)	Spontaneous, Specific Need
E-Mail (personalized)	"Think about this," Please Respond
Letter (handwritten)	Personal, Thoughtful, Warm
E-Mail (multiple recipients)	Less Personal, General Information Response Optional
Letter (typed)	Formal, General, Timeless
Memo	Institutional, General Information
Fax	Pertinent Information, Follow-up

This is obviously not an exact science, and there are certainly individual/corporate variations that can alter the application. However, I have learned that these apparently minor items, have a significant impact on determining the outcome of our interpersonal encounters.

On more than a few occasions I tried to address in an e-mail something I should have addressed in person. I have also created unnecessary anxiety and/or wasted time by scheduling a personal meeting with someone, when a phone call would have been sufficient.

As a result there are several factors I tried to keep in mind, especially as it related to assessing how personal the communication needed to be:

ACKNOWLEDGING PROBLEMS EARLY

- The more complicated, involved, or risky the information, the more personal the encounter needed to be.

- The newer the team member, the more personal the encounters needed to be.

- The more influential the team member, the more personal the communication should be.

Conversely, if the information was more straight-forward, or if there was a long-standing relationship, or if the person was not as *close* to the decision-making process, I felt greater freedom to move to less personal forms of communication.

GENDER COMPLICATIONS

I am not going to attempt to address the matter of women in leadership here. Regardless of a church's stance on this issue, we have all had to deal with the complications that arise from men and women relating closely in a ministry setting. Perhaps the first thing that needs to be said is that it *is* complicated. As a result, it regularly needs to be talked about. Unfortunately, in all too may places, it is not talked about often enough.

There are important reasons why we need to consider these relationships. We are all too familiar with the tragic experiences of churches that have had to suffer through the heartache of sexual infidelity among key players. The price it exacts from the people involved and the damage done to the reputation of these ministries, is nothing short of devastating. That, in itself, should keep us highly motivated to address this issue with diligence.

Creating reasonable relational boundaries between members of the opposite sex is critical. In order to pursue integrity within our particular organization, we operated under the following principles:

■ *Rules we abided by*

To maintain clarity and consistency, we agreed to the following
parameters for relating to members of the opposite sex:

- ◆ In counseling settings, our pastoral staff would not counsel a member of the opposite sex through long-term recov-
  ery. We limited ourselves to three sessions, and then
  referred them on.

- ◆ When we were meeting with a team member of the opposite sex at the office, we met with the door open or in a
  room with a window in the door.

- ◆ We didn't meet one-on-one with a member of the opposite sex, in their home, unless their spouse was present.

- ◆ We didn't go out to eat with a member of the opposite sex
  alone.

- ◆ We did not travel together alone with a member of the
  opposite sex.

- ◆ We had permission to check-up on each other and verify
  appointments.

At first, I must confess that I was resistant to this kind of rule-
intensive approach. I wanted to be more trusting. It seemed to me
that if people in the corporate world could meet/work together without having to create such restrictive boundaries, we as the church,
could be trusted to act responsibly. I soon realized that the issue was
rarely a matter of any individual team member's trustworthiness.

Not long after my sister moved to town, I took her out to dinner. The next day, when I got to the office, my Associate Pastor
pulled me aside. He told me that someone had called him the night
before with a grave concern regarding the integrity of the Senior
Pastor at Woodcrest. They had seen him in a dark corner of a

fancy restaurant with a beautiful blond. While my sister was flattered by the description, the incident only served to remind me of the fact that people were watching, and that those in ministry are held to a different standard. We could resent that and become bitter, or we could simply accept it as part of the environment we live in. Given the fact that people in our day are looking to discredit those in ministry, given the real temptations that need to be stringently avoided ... we found that these kind of relational boundaries were a reasonable concession.

■ Accountability that works

Even though I always had a high regard for the integrity and spiritual maturity of each of our team members, I was also acutely aware of the subtle and destructive tactics of the enemy of our faith. He is the one who is always seeking to disqualify those in Christian service. Sexual temptation seems to be one of his favorite ploys. For this reason, we were also enthusiastic advocates of the development of accountable relationships between team members. We found it wise to encourage each team member to have people in their lives who had permission to ask the harder questions.

Accountability that works is based on mutual trust and honesty. In our organization, while we required our team members to have accountable relationships, they had the prerogative to choose their own accountability partners, provided it was a member of the same sex.

Also, when we were dealing with a team member that was married, the health and strength of the marriage became a point of consideration as it related to the kind/amount of accountability expected. Obviously, that was a very sensitive issue, but the reality we faced, was that if a team member was in a difficult marital situation, their vulnerability required heightened accountability.

As important as these basic principles were, it would be irresponsible if we only thought in terms of illicit sexual behavior. This is a broad issue. It is also about understanding the challenge of emotional attachments, and being aware of the kinds of risks that ministry, by its very nature, places people in.

Ironically, the qualities that make us an effective team member/leader—a caring heart, a listening ear, an others-oriented disposition—are the very things that increase our vulnerability. In addition, there is always the risk of people being naive and self-deceived.

In an effort to develop some vocabulary that would help our team approach this otherwise ethereal area of concern, we created some categories to define the various ways we related to each other.

It was important to take the time to articulate these relational dynamics because it allowed us to do a better job at monitoring what was really happening in our hearts.

We used these tools primarily as a grid for self-assessment.

Professionalism		Favoritism
Affirmation		Flirtation
Complimentary partnerships		Unhealthy attachments
Attractive dress		Suggestive clothing
Reasonable amount of time together		Inordinate amount of time together
Proactive care and planning		Overindulgent preoccupation

They allowed us to take note of when we were moving into riskier territory. The pay off came when we dealt with these heart issues openly and honestly. We found we could then maximize the benefits of teamwork, and minimize the potential pitfalls.

In closing, the biggest hurdle that churches have to *get over* when it comes to addressing this issue, is the underlying assumption that any question we ask means that we are assuming the worst about one another. There is a prevailing sentiment that "mature" Christians don't need to worry about this kind of thing. That is often a smoke screen for our general unwillingness to deal with sensitive areas. I would be less than honest if I said that these are comfortable discussions. Even so, the risks of not addressing these matters are far more uncomfortable in the long run.

Ironically, the qualities that make an effective team member/leader—a caring heart, a listening ear, an others-oriented disposition—are the very things that increase one's vulnerability.

We need to have the courage to start somewhere—take a step, bring it up, and begin the process of tackling this critical area. It can literally make us or break us.

Now, on to something much more enjoyable!

THE BLESSING OF AFFINITY

At pastor's conferences and in seminary, much of the discussion regarding how to select appropriate staff (team members) centered around theological/doctrinal consistency, spiritual gifts, philosophic agreement and appropriate skill/experience. Without taking anything away from the value and necessity of each of these components, I felt disappointed by the fact that we rarely talked about the importance of interpersonal affinity, the value of working with people we genuinely like and appreciate. Perhaps this concept was seen as too mundane or unspiritual.

What really bothered me was the subtle suggestion that we should not work with people we like, because we'd be accused of recruiting a bunch of yes-men. With due consideration given to that possibility, we actually had the opposite experience. Relational affinity actually played a significant role in our team development.

In this chapter, we have been dealing with the subject of acknowledging and dealing with the problems. Let me build a case for how affinity makes that process easier. If churches grant team leaders permission to consider affinity as one of the qualifying characteristics for team members, here are a few of the benefits:

Increased Honesty — Contrary to conventional wisdom we can be more candid with people we like. While initially it might be difficult to test the boundaries of team relationship with *total* truth, in the end it actually solidifies the bond between us. We become more willing to engage in conflict, and more inclined to do the hard team-building *work*. Affinity then heightens security. If people feel secure in a relationship they are more willing to take the appropriate team-building risks.

Ease of Communication — When there were questions about the status of my relationship with someone, it complicated all my communication with them. I found myself much more measured in what I said. I listened critically to what they said and found myself wondering how I was being perceived. I would wonder . . . Is this conversation about *this subject*, or is it about something related to our relationship? On the other hand, when affinity was high, I was less inclined to worry about the sub-plots in our conversation, and it was easier just to say/accept things at face value.

How We Do Business Naturally — How does one select a restaurant? Typically, we consider the kind of food that is served or how far we have to drive. After that, we usually think of the kind of service we'll receive. I had a favorite lunch place not far from the office. The food was good, but the primary reason I went there was because I liked the wait staff. They smiled when I came in the door, they took time to ask about my family and work, and they were genuinely nice people. In fact, I chose to do all my business with people I like being around. Why should we operate differently in ministry?

Reason To Persevere — When we like working with someone, the sense of relational connectedness creates the incentive to work through the harder elements of team building. If there is little or no affinity, it won't be long before the relational maintenance will become the weight that tips the scale in favor of starting over with someone different. It really doesn't matter how talented that person is, or how long they have been part of the team, discontinuing the relationship will always seem more appealing when affinity is low. Conversely, there seems to be abundant grace and energy available for those we genuinely like.

Essential For Synergy — At their core, creative thinking and effective problem solving are mysterious art forms. We can talk at length about specific principles and tactics, but their application is generally governed by the depth of relationship shared by the participants. While this is difficult to explain, there is something truly magical that happens when affinity is added to the mix. We can have all the right ingredients—sharp minds, common purpose and spiritual maturity, yet without affinity the final outcome is rarely what we would have hoped for.

Heightened Joy Factor — Ministry is hard work. The fruit is often slow in coming and the weight of responsibility can be overwhelming. One of the few places we can find real soul satisfaction is in the relationships that are developed as we struggle through together. Giving team members permission to work alongside people they love is a reasonable—and I would suggest essential—element in making team life not only a way to do the work of ministry, but a way to be joyful in ministry.

I don't mean to suggest that affinity is the only, or even the most important thing to consider. Certainly skill, experience, maturity and heart are critical factors in hiring and recruiting. However, it is important to *acknowledge* that affinity is also a key component of team life. We need to understand that we all operate under the principle of affinity regardless of whether we discuss it openly or not. It is my contention that we need to give ourselves and our teams permission to consider affinity in the decision making process.

I had the chance, even as I wrote this book, to witness first hand the power of affinity. I wrote the first half of this book while on a sabbatical in Colorado. Every morning I would go to a donut shop, one that I soon discovered was the local hangout. On most mornings Teresa and Dana worked the counter. They were quite a team and really enjoyed themselves. They were gracious and kind to the customers—a good many of whom were a bit grumpy. Teresa had a hearty laugh that brightened up the whole place.

It was fascinating to watch them operate. There I was, sitting in their shop writing about teamwork, and as I was writing about it they were displaying it. I don't know what went on behind closed doors, but when they were on duty they produced like a great team. The coffee was fresh and there were plenty of fresh donuts in the display case (much to my chagrin). Despite the constant flow of traffic (and their children hanging on to their apron strings—literally) they seemed to have a way of giving every customer the individualized attention they needed.

I was pretty sure they didn't sit around in the back room philosophizing about teamwork. They simply enjoyed each other's company, and their affinity affected the whole environment. It was no wonder the place was so popular!

One morning when Teresa and Dana weren't working, I decided to visit another local establishment—a bagel shop up the street. It was empty, the gal on duty was sitting in the corner smoking a cigarette, and AC/DC was blaring on the radio. From the moment I walked in, I knew I had just interrupted her personal moment of silence. She got up to help me with a look that let me know she was not happy to do so. The location of this place was more convenient and the décor was more up-to-date than the donut shop. But, the feel was totally different. Maybe the key to good business isn't location, location, location—but affinity, affinity, affinity!

The contrast between these two experiences was so stark, that I was again convinced of the value of this basic principle of affinity. If we ignore it in ministry we do so to our own detriment.

CHAPTER SYNOPSIS

We see effective teams every where—in sports, in church, even at the local donut shop. When we note the synergy, relationships, and fruitfulness, there is something that rises up in all of us that says, "I want to be part of something like that!" These kind of teams are built by people who are ready and willing to do a lot of hard work, and much of that work is about dealing with problems—early and often.

♦ Let's be honest and deliberate in developing team relationships;

♦ Make a poster which states: There is no irreplaceable team member! Include ourselves;

- ◆ Share the final 10%, no matter what;

- ◆ Become adept at using qualifiers;

- ◆ Communicate the right meaning by employing the right means;

- ◆ Don't be naïve about relating to a member of the opposite sex;

- ◆ Enjoy the blessings of affinity. . . .

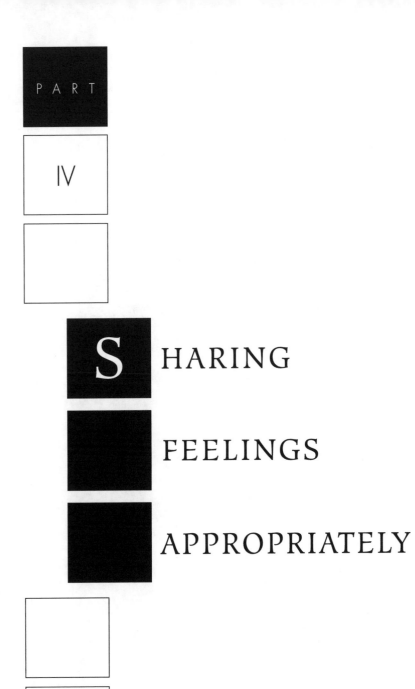

PART

IV

SHARING

FEELINGS

APPROPRIATELY

inistry is different.

I have worked in secular jobs and studied the world of business extensively, and I have discovered that ministry is indeed a unique vocation. Part of what makes it so unique is that in ministry, we bring our whole lives to work. In fact, it could be argued that the *best* ministries are those that stem from a genuine outgrowth of everything we are—our hearts, souls and minds. Certainly some might say that the same holds true for social services, medicine, education or even business. Yet as valuable and necessary as these professions are, in each of them, there is a clear distinction between personal and public life.

That is not to say that what a doctor, teacher, salesperson, or social worker does when they are off duty is irrelevant or inconsequential. In ministry however, our work is quite literally a product of who and what we are. There is no significant distinction between our home/private life, and our work life, because our home/private life is our first place of ministry.

To be clear, I am not suggesting ministers should be workaholics (although that is a very real temptation). Rather, ministry first and foremost is soul work—not just as it relates to other people's souls, but primarily as it relates to our own.

A minister with an empty and depleted soul is in reality not a minister at all. It may appear odd to see it put this way, but the chief objective in Christian service is to be a genuine Christian yourself first and always. Therefore, it is the primary responsibility of every minister to attend to his/her own soul first. When doing ministry as a team, we also have a responsibility to serve one another by attending to each other's soul development.

A minister *with an empty* *and depleted soul* *is in reality not a* *minister at all.* The reason I emphasize this so strongly is because there are cases where people in ministry attempt to make a private/public demarcation that is common to other professions. When this happens, a significant part of the ministerial calling is circumvented. More significantly, if private matters are not dealt with on the front end, then they will be dealt with on the back end, where it is always much harder.

There are certainly numerous stories of well-meaning and gifted ministers whose lives ended up in the ditch. Part of their lament seemed to be that they allowed the demands of ministry to dry up their soul. When we listen to their reflections on what happened, they testify repeatedly that if they had to do it over again, they would be much more diligent on the matter of personal soul development.

Over time, our organization developed some vocabulary that helped move us through this process with greater understanding. We will discuss these terms later in the chapter, but they will mean nothing if you don't buy into the process. For that reason, let's first discuss the foundational principles for dealing with and processing our emotions appropriately.

WHY THIS MATTERS SO MUCH

For much of 1999 there was a lively debate in our country about our President's immoral behavior with intern Monica Lewinsky. There wasn't much debate on whether or not what he/she did was wrong. Almost everyone was equally appalled by the actions. But there was significant discussion on the relevance of all this to his role as President.

On one hand, there were those who were saying that a person's private life had no bearing on their public performance. This President was presiding over a healthy economy, and many people felt like he was performing well in his position. His approval ratings hovered at about 70% throughout the scandal. The argument was consistently made that what consenting adults did behind closed doors was their own business.

On the other hand, there was a group saying that we couldn't make those kind of arbitrary distinctions between personal and private life, because character is foundational to leadership. If a man cheats on his wife, who's to say that he won't cheat on his country?

I don't want to get sidetracked by the specifics of this situation, but I do want to point out that the people who were most critical about Clinton's behavior were by and large Christian leaders or people with a strong sense of moral responsibility. People like Chuck Colson, Gary Bauer and William Bennett were very articulate in advocating that we cannot arbitrarily compartmentalize our lives.

If we have significant problems with our marriage or have problems with issues like sexual addiction, we are only fooling ourselves by saying that we can compensate for these weaknesses by trying to perform better on the job. The truth is that the secret things of life will always catch up with us—eventually. If we don't deal with the internal problems directly, those problems can and will shipwreck our lives no matter how much effort we give to other things.

Personally, I was very grateful for this debate, and was extremely impressed with the way that many Christians made their point. I also find it ironic that many of us can be guilty of

that same kind of thinking when it comes to the matter of dealing with our own *stuff*. Emotions are messy. We don't really like
dealing with them directly, so we'd rather compensate by working harder/longer on ministry activities.

Ironically, our thinking is amazingly similar to Clinton's in this
way. We assume that if we just focus on external ministry responsibilities such as preaching, visiting, and building the ministry, then
we won't have to deal with our internal emotional issues. We
compensate for our discomfort with the emotional side of life by
assuming that if we can stay active and aggressive in ministry, we
won't have to deal with any of it.

Doesn't the same advice we heard and gave in the political arena
apply here as well? We can't run from the emotional side of life. We
can't say that unresolved emotional issues won't affect other areas of
our life and ministry. We can't dodge the eventual consequences of
stuffed emotions by trying to do well in ministry service. We have to
deal with the emotions, and we have to share feelings appropriately.

The fact is ministry, by its nature, is not just a spiritual endeav-
or. It is an emotional venture as well.

Some jobs are mentally challenging. Some jobs require significant physical strength. The helping professions, and ministry
in particular, are emotionally draining vocations. People getting
involved in ministry for the first time often tell me they have never
felt as emotionally spent as when they got started in ministry.

Think about what ministry often entails:

♦ Loving people whose lives are often very much in disarray—
  ministers are typically called upon as an absolute last resort—
  when everything and everyone else has failed.

♦ Telling people about personal changes that are very difficult
  to make, often ministers are one of the few people that will
  be truly honest with those who need help.

+ Coming to grips with our own brokeness at the same time that we are trying to proclaim the truth and be strong for others.

+ Balancing a myriad of expectations about what the ideal minister should be, every person who comes to the church has a different set of ideas about what matters most.

+ Dealing with the fact that life change is slow, and that there are often, as many (if not more), disappointments as there are successes.

+ Beating back the personal attacks of the enemy who regularly plays on our insecurities and magnifies our mistakes.

+ Working through the financial woes that are regularly part of the mix, both at the church and in the home.

+ Accepting the fact that we cannot make everyone happy.

+ Juggling personal and family responsibilities with a job that is quite literally never really finished.

Obviously, these challenges require a measure of spiritual maturity, and because we are in ministry we are generally attuned to the need for adequate spiritual strength. However, we tend not to be as aware of how these challenges affect our emotions.

The emotional drain of ministry demands can catch us off guard, and we often don't know what to do with all our conflicting feelings. Some of us, who have been around ministry for a while, can lose sight of how intense this whole process really is. We can easily forget how important it is to process feelings appropriately. Team ministry can further complicate the matter because we have to deal with a whole group of people trying to figure it out at the same time. Therefore, unless we create the vocabulary and safe environments for this kind of emotional processing "Clintonesque" scandals will continue to plague the church as well.

So, what does this mean in terms of our daily routine?

REGULAR CHECK-INS

Most of our meetings began with a time of checking in. That time was devoted to personal sharing. It included a time of reporting on what was taking place in our devotional lives, family experiences, and/or personal processing. Usually this check-in period didn't take but a few minutes. The value was found in the fact that we regularly affirmed the importance and relevance of what was happening with us personally.

I remain convinced that the check-in times did, on several occasions, salvage the spiritual integrity of various team members. Another side benefit was the enhanced team and relational development. However, the procedure for creating these kind of safe environments and balancing ministry production with personal processing always took effort and energy to structure efficiently.

FEELINGS AND TRUTH

Because many Christians seem especially uncomfortable with their emotions, we quickly want to move to what we *should* do, or how we *should* feel, and we don't take the time to work through the root issues. The fact that there is no clear direction in the Bible on this issue makes it even more difficult.

In fact, I was in a pastor's meeting, where we discussed avoiding ministry burnout. A highly respected pastor said, "I'm not sure this is something we should spend any time talking about because I've never read the word *burnout* in the Bible."

Part of what this pastor may have been reacting to was the tendency for some of us to elevate feelings over truth. In other words, in some circles we may have spent so much time sorting through emotional issues, that by virtue of the time spent on it, it would appear that emotional matters (subjective reality) are more important than matters of truth (objective reality). Certainly, those risks exist when we give people permission to process their emotional baggage. However, the answer to this is quite simple: Always process emotions on the basis of truth or alongside truth.

In other words, we made the agreement as a ministry team, that we would live our lives on the basis of God's truth. We would not be subject to fleeting emotions of the moment and allow them to govern our life—but we would act and live according to God's principles. Once we had set that out as our goal, then there was no argument about where we were headed, and we could process our emotions with a clear understanding of the final objective.

Perhaps, you're wondering how this actually plays itself out in a meeting, or in conversation between team members. Let me illustrate by sharing some common scenarios.

Let's imagine that we are on a team, and we're reviewing an event or a service. Part of the agenda is to give feedback on what took place at the event. Perhaps we felt like some important things were missed in the event, and that other things could have been done better. These comments are hard to make and we may find ourselves concerned with how our comments will be received . . . and how we will be perceived. What do we do? One side of our brain argues that we need to say something because it is our job. The other side of us argues that we shouldn't say anything because it might hurt someone's feelings.

Or, let's say we have a question about why a decision was made. We have been told that the reason for the decision was about *this* and *that*, but we *feel* like there may be more to it. We don't want to be accusatory. We don't want to come across as untrusting or suspicious. How do we express what we feel without communicating it in a way that damages the emotions of the rest of the team?

Many of us choose one of two options:

1. *Ignore the feelings and just do what's right* — We don't want to worry about the emotional outcomes. We think to ourselves that others need to be less sensitive. We proudly think that our feelings never keep us from doing the right thing ... if that's a problem for someone else, it's hardly our responsibility.

2. *Let the feelings control us and keep us from doing the right thing* — We can't risk offending someone, because people are more important than tasks. So, if we are at risk of hurting people's feelings, we shouldn't do it.

Neither of those options is acceptable, and if we live in either realm it will do very little to enhance the sense of teamwork. Instead, the challenge is to understand that there are always two realities, and both of them need to be taken seriously. The danger lies in ignoring one or the other.

Perception is Reality: Perceptions deal primarily with the world of feelings and impressions.

and

Reality is Reality (too): When we are talking about reality in this way, we are talking about the world of principles and truth.

Ignoring either world can cause real trouble, not only for ourselves but also for the team. In our context, we found it most helpful to deal with each *reality* separately. In other words, if we were in a conversation about something that we knew would be sticky, and we had a lot of emotions running wild inside us, we would begin by addressing those fears first.

We might have said it like this, "I have to talk about perceptions first. I am feeling as though there is something going on here that I don't completely understand. I may have no logical reason to believe this, but I am concerned that if I share what is really on my heart, you might not hear me . . . . I need to process these feelings, because I am hoping to sort out the truth from fiction first, then we can talk about the other stuff."

Once we processed the perceptions, then we could move to truth with greater confidence and relational security. The truth elements could be dealt with on their own merits, without the typical questions of "what is this *really* about." In fact, sometimes we could actually be less articulate about truth concerns and still be better understood, simply because there were no hidden agendas. Once the concerns stemming from perception were on the table the typically unspoken distractions no longer needed to enter into the discussion—they had already been dealt with. As a result, people were free to focus on the more substantive issues.

Let's not grow up to become embittered leaders who are just going through the motions of church life.

I can imagine that some might feel like this is quite unnecessary. Why would anyone want to go through all this? It does appear very time-consuming, and it may seem to take valuable time away from doing what needs to be done. I understand this tension, as it can feel very laborious and overdone. I have sat in meetings that seemed to go on and on, simply because someone had to process their emotions. However, the value over the long haul was significant, because the effort was fundamentally about protecting and preserving our hearts—and that is something the Bible challenges us to address as a priority.

Above all else guard your heart,
for it is the well spring of life.

Proverbs 4:23

When we fail to deal responsibly with our feelings, one of things that happens is that our hearts tend to shrink and shrivel.

Our heart can become embittered and hard. We can no longer trust. We can become angry and resentful.

One of the saddest testimonies of the Church today is that there are long time church members whose hearts are no longer big for people or for God. This state of affairs has always saddened me because their crankiness is typically not a product of their aging bodies. It is not because they don't know enough about the Bible. Rather, it is because they have been hurt in some way, and instead of dealing with the feelings appropriately, they allowed them to fester.

The end result is always the same—Shrinking Heart Syndrome!

Do any of us really want to end up living that way? Is that the legacy we want to leave for our children? Do we really want to find ourselves at the end of our lives with small shriveled up hearts—where we don't care much for people or for God? Let's not grow up to become embittered leaders who are just going through the motions of church life.

If that is our goal, we must continue to force ourselves to go through the laborious processing of emotions. As much as it depends on us, we should give each team member the opportunity to look forward to a future filled with a greater love for God and a stronger heart for people.

CONNECTING THE DOTS

Emotions have been given to us to help us understand the things going on inside of us. In the same way that our capacity to feel (on a physical level) protects us from injury and warns us of potential physical over-extension, our capacity to feel (on an emotional level) is one of the God-given ways to assess the state of our soul.

Those of us who may not be adept at processing our emotions, may have a more difficult time managing our soul. Sometimes pastoral and psychiatric care can help us get past emotional barriers, but we can also become more skilled in deciphering what is going on inside of us. If we are tuned-in to *what* we are feeling and *why* we might be feeling it, we can become much more productive. Understanding the connection between the *what* and the *why* is critical, and it involves awareness and skill on two different levels.

1. To know *what* I'm feeling has to do with my capacity to accurately define my emotional state in any given circumstance.

2. To know *why* I'm feeling that way has to do with my capacity to understand how my feelings are linked to past experiences and/or personality strengths and weaknesses.

On the surface this may sound fairly straightforward, but the truth is, there are often numerous limitations and problems that arise on both sides of this equation. We may want to work on these things, and we may even have some clues about what may be going on behind the scenes. But we often lack perspective. Therefore, it isn't uncommon for people to get stuck on the specifics.

The cycle looks something like this:

ON IDENTIFYING WHAT WE'RE FEELING

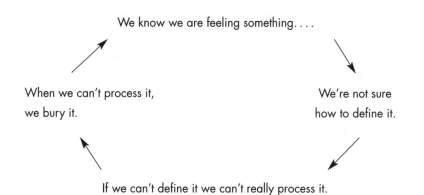

We know we are feeling something. . . .

When we can't process it, we bury it.

We're not sure how to define it.

If we can't define it we can't really process it.

As this cycle continues, it isn't long before we end up being ruled by emotions that we don't understand and can't get past. By stopping long enough to pay attention to what is really going on we can begin to reverse the cycle.

We reach an important developmental milestone when we have the capacity to identify feelings and not ignore, minimize or spiritualize what is going on within us. This involves stopping and actually taking the time to figure out what we're feeling. This is especially important when we are endeavoring to process our negative emotions—feelings of anger, disappointment, rejection, sadness, regret, etc.

> *We reach an important developmental milestone when we have the capacity to identify feelings and not ignore, minimize or spiritualize what is going on within us.*

Once we get better at identifying the kind of emotions we are feeling, the next question we need to address is to discover *why* are we feeling that way.

Sometimes this is pretty simple, but there are times when we have an emotional reaction to an event that seems disproportionate with the situation. It is as though we "pulled out a shotgun to kill the mosquito."

For example, an assignment in the portfolio of one of our team members was reassigned to another person. The team leader thought she was simply evening out workloads, and matching projects with people's gifting and schedule. It seemed like a totally logical move in her mind. The team leader actually expected the team members to be grateful for the sensitivity and care she had demonstrated.

What happened however, was that the team member who lost the assignment was quite upset about the transfer of responsibility. He felt cheated out of something important. From the team leader's perspective, the amount of disappointment expressed seemed out of sync with the magnitude of the decision. At that point, it would have been very easy for the team leader to shut down the process by responding harshly to the team member. But in so doing an important learning opportunity would have been lost.

When the team leader took time to explore what was behind the disappointment, she discovered something significant. In previous environments in which this team member worked, communication was never very open. Bosses expressed their displeasure in subtle and indirect ways. Employees weren't told directly that they weren't measuring up to expectations. Instead, they were moved out of the loop and given less and less responsibility, until it was clear that were no longer wanted or needed. In the end, people would leave because they were tired of feeling so ostracized.

By entering our ministry context this team member was hoping for something different, yet wasn't really sure how he would be received. The early shuffling of responsibilities raised fears that perhaps he was going to experience the same thing all over again. Sub-consciously, the team member assumed that the leader was already losing trust in his capacity to serve effectively, and that this project transfer was just the first step toward an inevitable demotion or dismissal. After finding that out, the leader was able to reiterate the real reasons for the transfer. She also took the opportunity to quell the fears of the team member, and reaffirm his value as a significant player on the team.

On the surface, this may sound trivial, but perhaps the importance of these interactions can be best understood when we consider what happens when we *don't* take the time. When these emotions aren't processed, when teams don't work through the *whats* and the *whys* of their feelings, then the emotions build up as a potentially destructive force just below the surface. They fester and increase in intensity, and over time they can create a significant challenge that can have disastrous long-term ramifications. What is more amazing is that one simple thirty-minute conversation can diffuse what might otherwise turn into a debilitating showdown.

These kind exchanges require a willingness and openness on the part of both team leaders and team members. The responsibilities and challenges, however, are slightly different for each. Let's take a look at how these things play out uniquely for team leaders and team members.

THE DISCIPLINE OF LEADERS

Typically, leaders feel the greatest weight of ministry production. The hard thing about Sundays is that they come around with amazing regularity. Whether we are planning a service, a children's program, or an adult study group, there are a myriad of things that need to get done before every service/event/group takes place. Every week, there is a job to do and it simply *has* to get done.

If there is a team involved in the planning and implementation process, the team leader is always juggling multiple responsibilities:

+ Have the agenda ready (know what needs to be accomplished, and be ready to explain it to the rest of the team).

+ Be sensitive to the other team members' time and schedule (be responsible to start and end on time).

+ Encourage the participation of each team member (endeavoring to balance gifting, availability, and personal interests).

+ Plan and produce something that is fresh and of high-quality (because whatever you do, you want it to reflect well on the Lord, the church and the team).

The ministry task is critical. Leaders cannot imagine shrinking back from the importance of making sure ministry *happens*.
That is what makes this idea of emotional processing so difficult.
It seems to fly in the face of getting the job done. To risk not getting part of the ministry assignment accomplished in order to
attend to a team member's feelings can seem on the verge of irresponsible.

Even so, here's how we should think about it:

▲ *The team is the leader's first place of ministry* — Ironically,
around the church, we can think of ministry as something for
"those people out there." Yet the truth is, ministry begins at
the place of closest influence. Jesus certainly alluded to that
kind of prioritization in the way that he sent out the disciples.

> . . . and you will be my witnesses in Jerusalem, and in all Judea
> and Samaria, and to the ends of the earth.
>
> Acts 1:8

Ministry, for the disciples, began in their hometown of
Jerusalem. Their ministry in Jerusalem set them up for broader influence. In the same way, it is a leader's ministry to his or
her "home team" that sets the team up for broader influence
in the church.

▲ *Ministry is about people* **and** *product* — Sometimes ministries
or churches get sidetracked by the fruitless argument of what
matters most: the people doing the ministry or the ministry
those people produce? It is unequivocally both! Once we decide
to prioritize one above the other, we risk losing something very
important—namely the people or the product. Certainly there
are times when one area might need additional attention or
emphasis, but they are both always equally important. Over
the life of the team, both sides need consistent and diligent

effort. The leader is the primary catalyst in creating the environment that gives permission for this kind of dual focus.

▲ *Healthy teams create healthy ministry* — This may sound obvious, but it bears mentioning, because we often act and think in a way that is contrary to this principle. We want to believe that we can produce ministry that is better or different from what we are like. For example, if a team is insensitive, duplicitous, and unfocused, it is impossible for this team to create something compassionate, consistent, and focused. Teams produce ministry that is of a nature and character that is congruent with who and what we are. The Biblical principle is drawn from a lesson in nature.

> *My brothers, can a fig tree bear olives, or a grapevine bear figs?*
> *Neither can a salt spring produce fresh water.*
>
> James 3:11

Again, the leader's role in facilitating the character of the team is essential. The axiom, "speed of the leader—speed of the team" is applicable here.

THE COMMITMENT OF TEAM MEMBERS

In much of the literature on teamwork, there is a subtle (and sometimes not so subtle) inference made that teams don't really need leaders. The suggestion is made that on the best kind of teams there is no need for a designated leader. Instead, authority should be equally shared among all the team members. In our democratic (and sometimes even anti-authority) culture the "everyone is the same" philosophy sounds very appealing. However, in practice, leaderless teams are rarely very effective.

In addition, the scriptures designate the role of leadership as critical in the life of the church. According to Romans 12, leadership is included in the list of spiritual gifts. Hebrews 13 reminds us to remember our leaders, and follow their example. Later in that same chapter, we are even admonished to obey and submit to our leaders. Finally, just by the sheer power of example, the Bible illustrates God's apparent preference to work in and through leaders to accomplish his work.

Due to various public displays of abuse in leadership, we tend to be very cautious about following any leader. Understandable. Yet consider the blessings of being well led:

- The vision and mission is clear.
- Resources are leveraged for maximum impact.
- Team members feel valued and appreciated for their individual contributions.
- Problems and difficulties are addressed openly and honestly.
- Victories are celebrated regularly and enthusiastically.

Conversely, consider what typically happens when leadership is inept and/or non-existent:

- The vision and mission is consistently unclear or always changing.
- Financial and personnel resources are poorly managed.
- Team members rarely feel acknowledged or valued.
- Problems go unresolved, and the team can be thwarted by unhealthy conflict.
- Victories are few and far between, and when they do occur they are not celebrated.

Good leadership makes a significant difference in the life of teams. The quality of the leadership experience is at least partly driven by the environment that the members help create. Our willingness to respond appropriately to leadership can often determine the team's capacity to experience genuine fruitfulness. This is especially important when discussing the matter of processing emotions, for under the guise of sharing feelings team members can actually undermine the role of the leader.

Here were a few mutually agreed upon commitments that our team members made:

Remember who's the leader — Leading teams is hard enough as it is. Therefore, in order not to complicate matters, there was no arguing about the importance or necessity of legitimate leadership authority. Without taking anything away from *losing, acknowledging* and *sharing,* it was important to remember that the role of the leader merited a basic honor and respect that would affect the way team members prayed, acted, and spoke.

Don't share a frustration without bringing a solution — Instead of sharing frustrations, disappointments, and/or problems with the expectation that the leader or rest of the team would solve them, every team member was asked to take the initiative. They brought a possible solution at the same time they brought up their concern. It didn't even have to be a good solution. It was simply important that team members stayed proactive in bearing some of the responsibility in addressing their issues, whether that issue was corporate or personal in nature.

Any demand must be accompanied with a resignation — A demand placed upon a team or team leader was a serious thing. Demands are manipulative. When someone said, "This *must* happen . . ." the very next statement needed to be, "I am willing to tenure my resignation if necessary." We said this not because we wanted to create an environment where threats were common place. Rather, we wanted to do the opposite. We wanted each team member to be circumspect about the way they made demands of the team.

COMMUNITY VERSUS THERAPY

One final caveat on this matter of sharing feelings. Part of the justification for processing emotions (as a team) is the hope that this kind of sharing is not only helpful to the person sharing, but that it also builds the sense of community on the team. However, there comes a point where the kind of sharing that we are describing crosses a line (albeit fuzzy and inexact) where a team member is no longer in need of deeper community, the person is in need of therapy. I say that with no jest or malice intended.

Therapy can be a very important part of a person's journey toward healthy ministry. Therefore, when the need for emotional processing moved beyond the bounds of team-building community, we encouraged people to pursue the professional help they really needed. A friend of mine, Rick McGinniss (Pastor of North Heartland Community Church in Kansas City), developed a list of characteristics that may help people discern when they have crossed the community/therapy threshold.

Teams produce ministry that is of a nature and character that is congruent with who and what we are.

We have an irrational dread over doing ministry.

> It's not fun anymore.

> We don't look forward to doing what we used to love doing.

> We don't like being around the people we serve or who serve with us.

We have constant anxiety about new challenges.

› When something unexpected happens we have an impending sense of doom.

› We feel butterflies in our stomach every time someone says, "Oh did you know that such and such didn't work out?" or, "we've got a problem with so and so."

We are overwhelmed by thoughts of "it's all up to me."

› We continue to believe that if we don't do it, it won't get done.

› We are convinced nobody else cares like we do.

We are plagued by nagging doubts of "I'm not good enough"

› After we've seen God use us, and our calling is secure, we start losing our confidence anyway.

› We start believing that we're no longer adequate for the task.

› We start imagining that other people are out to take our job

We display hypersensitivity to minor criticisms.

› We over-react to suggestions

› We think that every comment has a deeper hidden meaning

› We lash out, pout, or seek other unhealthy ways to mend wounds

We experience extended periods where it is difficult to sense God's presence.

› We're so busy helping other people sense God's presence, but we can't connect with God ourselves.

› All we can think about is the next task.

We can't relax when we're off.

› When we get a little down time—instead of resting, our brain is thinking about the things that still need our attention.

> We're constantly jumping in to put out fires that somebody else can/should handle—even when we should be replenishing

We experience little or no joy in God or His blessings.

> We have an inability to "rejoice," as Jesus said, "over the fact that your name is written in the Lamb's book of Life." (Luke 10:20)

> We can no longer rejoice over the fact that "every good and perfect gift is from above, coming down from the Father of Lights." (James 1:17)

We continue to think, "I'm too busy (or tired) to spend time with God."

> It's like the old story about the guy who was chopping furiously at a tree, but he made little progress. His neighbor came along and said, "It might be a lot easier if you sharpened that axe you're using," to which the man replied, "I can't. I'm too busy chopping trees."

We settle for spiritual "junk food."

> We put the mind and body on the path of least resistance.

> We turn to TV, eating, video games or surfing the net to feed our soul, instead of reconnecting with God and others in Christian community.

CHAPTER SYNOPSIS

Dealing with the emotional side of team development can be one of the most challenging parts of team life. Therefore, be vigilant!

♦ Recognize and appreciate ministry's uniqueness;

- Understand the risk of avoiding emotional issues by diverting attention to ministry issues;

- Engage in regular team check-ins;

- Differentiate between perceptions and reality;

- Work hard at identifying what we're feeling and why we're feeling it;

- If we're team leaders remember our priorities;

- If we're team members be mindful of our commitments;

- Be clear on the signals that show when we have moved from the need for community to the need for therapy.

TAKING

BOTH

SIDES

I n some ways this section will seem at odds with what we have talked about in the previous chapters. So far, I have been encouraging the process of taking the initiative, engaging the conflict, sharing the feelings and confronting the problems.

In this chapter, I will address another side of team building. This concept, though equally important, will feel much more passive. It is about accepting the limitations and personality quirks of our team members. Some of what we find objectionable about team members and/or team leaders are things that are basic to that person's personality and style. The hard truth here is, that no matter how much we talk, converse or confront we are not going to make headway. Whatever we are addressing is part of *who they are*.

THE "COIN" PRINCIPLE

Just like every coin has two sides, so it is with every personality type. There may be some people on our team who we recruited because of their attention to detail, their capacity to understand and enforce policy, and their sensitivity to fairness and equity. When that person joins the team, what are we saying about them?

I remember when we brought a new financial director on staff. She was highly qualified (CPA) and she had a real heart for ministry. When she came on board we were singing her praises. We rolled out the red carpet and said things like:

"We are so glad that you are here . . ."
"Nobody has cared as much about this kind of thing before . . ."
"We need people like you to help us get/stay organized . . ."
"God has sent you to us . . .

Let's roll the clock ahead six months, can you guess what people were saying about this same person around the office?

"This person is so obsessive . . ."
"They nit-pick about everything . . ."
"Where did all these forms come from . . . ?"

What happened? Did this God-sent person change suddenly? No, we were simply looking at the other side of the coin! This kind of thing happens all the time, on every team. Unless we are aware of it, it can truly frustrate the process.

Most ministers have had to deal with this same issue in premarital counseling. In the first session with a couple we might begin by talking about what it was that drew the two people together. She might say:

"I love the fact that he is such hard worker."
"I love that he never seems to get flustered by anything."
"I love that he is such a good listener."

And he might respond:

"I love that she takes such an interest in my life."
"I love how she cares deeply about what happens to others and how compassionate she is."
"I love that she is not afraid to tell me about whatever is on her mind."

It is always difficult to cast a ripple of disturbance upon the smooth waters of such perfect harmony in a young couple, but we as pastors must, for it is our responsibility to encourage couples to consider fully the qualities they admire in each other. We need to say to them, "In a sense, you are choosing not only the qualities you love in each other but the qualities you dislike—but feel you can deal with." For example, we might say to her, "Consider some of the possible flip sides of the qualities you admire in him and how you might respond to them in the future:

"You respect his hard-working attitude, but hard workers can also have trouble relaxing from work—suppose you eventually become troubled by his inability to take time off from work."

or

"You appreciate his steadiness, but this is a quality that can also result in insensitivity at times."

or

"You value his capacity to listen, but good listeners often have difficulty sharing their thoughts and feelings, and this might begin to disturb you over time."

Then we might say to him:

"You appreciate her interest in your life and her desire to see you succeed, but people change over time and you might come to experience this as pressure and intrusiveness."

or

"You appreciate her compassion and depth of feeling, but compassionate people tend to be highly sensitive and often emotional, and you might come to find her responses to people and situations to be excessive."

or

"You love her capacity to share what is on her mind, but if you are not this way yourself, you might eventually find it diffcult to participate in this degree of conversation."

Of course we cannot make predictions, but years of pastoral experience reveal the principle of the coin—the dual nature of our strengths and our weaknesses.

The same thing plays out with churches too. I was having breakfast with another pastor in our community, a pastor whose church was far different from our own:

Our church was very informal — They were very formal, everybody dressed up, and he preached in a robe.

Our church was young and transient — They had a sense of stability, where everybody knew each other.

Our Sunday morning services were oriented toward the disenchanted and made extensive use of drama, music, and video — Their services were oriented toward the maturing believer, and they used the great Christian traditions of hymns, creeds and responsive readings.

Our building looked like a warehouse — They met in a beautiful sanctuary with stained glass windows, crosses, altars, and a choir loft.

As we sat over breakfast we talked of some people who had left our church to go to his. They had left ours because we were "too informal," "too contemporary," "the building itself is just too plain."

At the conclusion of our conversation, I had to laugh because part of the reason he wanted to meet with me was because these same folks that had just left our church to attend his, were already expressing concerns about the ministry—and guess what the complaints centered around?

"A little too stiff . . . "

"A little too traditional . . . "

"Can't we try something new every now and again . . . ?"

Every time we declare something that we are, we are also declaring what we are not! We can't do/be everything. This is the great illusion that keeps so many of us unhappy. We think we can have or be it all. Interestingly enough, we may even say, "The problem is that we're just not enough like Jesus, because if we were more like him then we wouldn't have to face these issues."

Obviously if we were all mimicking Christ's maturity, love and passion, then things really would be better. What about the coin? Is the dual nature of people and situations really something we wouldn't have to deal with if we were more Christ-like? If so, that would mean that Jesus was beyond the "coin principle," or that the coin doesn't apply to him. Consider this:

What is it that we love about Jesus?

— He cares about those outside the family of God—they merit an all out search.

— He speaks the truth, he never lies—he *is* the truth!

— He always invites us to take the next step—pressing us to grow and mature.

Why do we sometimes have trouble with Jesus?

— He cares deeply about seekers (and expects us to as well).

— He claims to be the truth, and there is no truth outside him.

— He expects us to grow, and puts us in situations to ensure that we do.

The inescapable fact remains that the coin applies across the board.

THE TRUTH ABOUT THOSE WE LOVE . . .

What makes this whole idea even more complicated is that the 80% we love about each other is actually driven by the 20% we hate. In other words, it's not just that we have a coin, but the flip side of the coin is often what inspires the things we love. Sometimes we find ourselves saying that if a particular team member would just change ... then he or she would be great to work with. In actuality, if somehow we could change them, we would very quickly discover that we wouldn't have the same person. More importantly, we wouldn't be happy with the result.

If we could get rid of what we hate we would lose what we love as well.

How do we deal with this reality?

■ Understand that this is reality!

Because this is reality, we have to understand that we have choices. We have to make decisions not only about what we want, but what we can stand to live with—knowing that whatever comes on one side has another side too—and both sides are part of the package.

One of my favorite Old Testament passages is found in Joshua 24:15. It is a verse where Joshua draws a line in the sand. In the first part of the chapter, he spends time reviewing what God has done, what He expects, and what it means to follow Him. Then he says,

"Choose today whom you will serve ... "

Joshua is clear about what is at stake. Following God's truth includes multiple blessings. It also means abiding by certain rules, values and ideals. The promised blessing comes with the corresponding restrictions. If we want the blessing we must accept the restrictions.

The same is true with people and teams. I had a choice about who I wanted to work with, and everything about who they were came with them. I may not have liked everything about them, but I had to take the bad with the good. I had to accept the reality of the coin. Waiting for an option that involved no flip side was an illusion. The only question left to ask was, what flip side was I willing to live with?

■ *Understand and accept people's flip side*

One of the best places to start working through these issues is to anticipate what the flip side might look like. Since we all have a flip side, our ability to work with others hinges (at least partly) on our capacity to recognize and embrace people's entire coin. Here is a good question to ask regularly, "What is it about our team members that we love?"

- Do we love their creativity?
- Do we love their willingness to help?
- Do we love the fact that they make sure things are done right?
- Do we love their easy going and fun loving ways?

Guess what? Whatever it is that we love about these people has a side that will drive us crazy. What makes matters worse is that their flip side is what inspires their positive side. Consider the flip side of the aforementioned characteristics:

POSITIVE SIDE   FLIP SIDE

Creativity ←——————————————— Unorthodox

Helpfulness ←——————————————— Controlling

Excellence ←——————————————— Perfectionism

Playfulness ←——————————————— Irreverence

Attention to ←——————————————— Compulsive
detail

The apostle Paul spent a lot of time writing about interpersonal relationships. In Romans 14, he begins by reviewing things that people tend to argue about in the church. He then goes on to give his readers a few principles on how to deal with these differences. He closes his instructions with an appeal for believers to be committed to the unity of the body of Christ.

In Romans 15, he begins by laying the groundwork for that unity. He writes,

> *Accept each other as Christ has accepted you* . . . .

Romans 15:7

F. F. Bruce, in his commentary on Romans suggests that the word "acceptance" is probably better translated as *welcomed*, because this is something we should do for each other willingly. Acceptance tends to communicate a resolved but reluctant acquiescence. But it's clear from the context that Paul sets the standard high, in the same way that the Lord has accepted/welcomed us *coin and all*—we should similarly welcome one another.

■ Building teams with the flip side in mind

What gets us in trouble is either: (a) a personal unwillingness to acknowledge the reality of our own coin, or (b) the minimization of a team member's flip side. The result is that teams can be built with gaps, lapses, and blind spots.

The scriptures describe the church by comparing her to a human body. One of the characteristics of a human body is that it has different parts, each with a different function, and those functions are complimentary.

> *Under his direction, the whole body is fitted together perfectly. As each part does its own special work, it helps the other parts grow, so that the whole body is healthy and growing and full of love.*

Ephesians 4:16 (NLT)

It is important to stay positive in our evaluation of the coin principle. Instead of seeing the coin as a primarily negative thing, we found it best to celebrate team members' strengths and bring others in to compensate for the flip sides.

REASONABLE ADJUSTMENTS

It is important to use caution in discussing the coin principle. There can be a tendency to become resistant to making reasonable adjustments in our behavior because we feel justified in our reactions ..." See I'm just *this way*, and there is nothing I (or any one else) can do about it!" There may also be hesitancy in dealing with inappropriate behavior from others on the team. This can stem from a resigned sense that we have to tolerate the flip side.

For this reason, it is vital that we work through the finer nuances with a good measure of maturity and discernment. We all have a responsibility—if for no other reason than to grow and mature ourselves—to address the negative ramifications of our coin. For example, a team member's compulsive tendencies may make them very good at managing the details, but if their compulsive behavior becomes such an interpersonal irritant that no one wants to work with them any more, both the team member and the organization loses out.

Every time we declare something that we are, we are also declaring what we are not!

Our financial director (who I mentioned earlier) was a quick study on all this. She understood the climate of our organizational environment and the limitations of our staff. She was also patient about the process of implementing her new procedures. Her flip side could have become a major stumbling block to the staff's willingness to move to new levels of financial accountability. That didn't happen, because she was mature enough to process her frustrations in appropriate ways. She didn't take the staff's hesitation/reluctance as a personal affront. Her example has provided an illustration of how we can mitigate the down side of our flip side.

Be aware of our flip side — Understand how, why, and when it manifests itself. Sometimes we think that personal introspection has little value, and though there are those that can be obsessively pre-occupied with personal evaluation, this is one area where accurate self-awareness is critical.

Have a few safe confidantes — We all need a couple of people around us who love us enough to give us honest feedback, individuals who will tell us how we are coming across and the ways in which it is difficult for others to receive us. They can also provide the needed opportunities to vent our disappointments and frustrations.

Love for the people and the place — If we are going to endure the hardships associated with processing our own flip side, and if we are going to deal with the ways that we are frustrated by others, we need to love the people around us and believe in the purposes we are jointly committed to.

Don't take things personally — One of the ways a situation can deteriorate quickly is if we become hyper-sensitive about decisions in our areas of responsibility. We can't assume that if something happens contrary to our wishes, that it automatically signals some kind of personal affront. There is an old adage that bears repeating, *you wouldn't worry so much about what people thought about you if you realized how much they didn't.*

Pray for the tempering work of God's Spirit — God knows how to protect that which is precious and refine that which is destructive. He promises to complete the work that he has begun in us. We should regularly give God permission to know and develop our hearts. With the Psalmist, let us pray,

Create in me a clean heart O God,
Renew a right spirit within me . . .

Psalm 51:10

CHAPTER SYNOPSIS

Working and ministering with different kinds of people presents a host of interesting challenges. Some experiences are truly exhilarating, while others are down-right depressing. When we are working with a team, the people we know best can present some of our greatest challenges. We see them up close. We are aware of their strengths and contributions, but their weaknesses are equally obvious. Understanding how and why such stark contrasts can exist within the same person helps us to accept them.

- Every person, like every coin, has two sides;

- The truth about those we love is: if we take away what irritates us, we may lose what we cherish as well;

- Simply because we have a flip side, it doesn't mean we should stop growing and improving;

- When building a team, build it with the flip side in mind . . . .

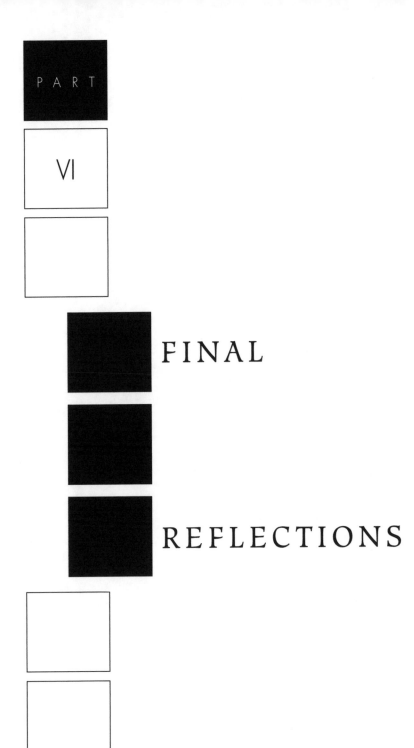

PART

VI

FINAL

REFLECTIONS

T hroughout these pages, I have described the practices that have become core to our understanding of how teams work best. These practices were not discovered in an ivory tower, nor were they the product of extensive literary research. Rather, these practices came from the front lines of ministry activity. They were learned in the school of practical experience, where we kept what worked and discarded what didn't.

Part of what is lost in the communication via book form is the tremendous amount of trial and error that we engaged in. It is difficult to account for every mistake and change in a manuscript—it wouldn't make for enjoyable reading either. Defining and describing the principles necessitated summarizing.

Therein lies the challenge for teams reading this material. Any time people learn about a new ministry practice—especially if it is laid out using an acronym—it can *seem* so simple. The initial thought might be, "This is going to be fairly easy. We'll just have a few meetings to talk about these ideas, and before long the new practices will be in place. The benefits will also come quickly."

It doesn't happen that way.

The more likely scenario is that you will discuss these ideas, and a few might even be tried. Things will not go as you hoped. As a result, you may come back to the drawing board and have another discussion, perhaps many long discussions. Only this time the conversations will be more candid. If you're lucky you might even address some root issues along the way.

A few of the team members may make a more concerted effort, and re-think how they structure their meetings and how they delegate/accept responsibility. A new level of sharing may take place in certain circles, but in other places people will still be somewhat suspicious and cautious. You'll have a few break-throughs and a few setbacks. Some on your team will have high hopes, others may think this is just another passing fad. Some may rise to new levels of enthusiasm and engagement, and others may decide they can't live up to the new expectations.

Building great teams is messy business.

So why go through the hassle? I've asked myself that same question many times. The answer I have given myself and others can appear overly simplistic at first glance, but it is the core moti-vation behind the writing of this book. Here it is: *When teams are working well, they exceed your expectations.* Shared workload, syn-ergistic creativity, relational satisfaction, complimentary special-ization, heightened effectiveness, and increased efficiency, are words and concepts that get thrown around a lot these days. Because of their over-use we can lose sight of their power and meaning. Yet, when you really begin to experience some of it—it is amazing how good it is. When a team is functioning like a team and not just called a team, it is pretty phenomenal. In fact, it makes all the hard work pale by comparison.

Woodcrest Chapel is located in a relatively small city in the middle of Missouri. No offense to the fine residents of Columbia, but the location was not necessarily one that brought big city resources crashing through our doorways. As a result, people often asked me how we were able to recruit the tremendous talent that we had at Woodcrest. Our talent was drawn from places like Dal-las, Texas and San Diego, California—locations far more exotic than mid-Missouri. If you talked to the recruits themselves each of them would tell you the very same thing. The appeal of Woodcrest was in the strength and vitality of the ministry team. It was what drew them, and it was what kept them.

When you consider how valuable it is for a strong team to come together to do ministry, and to do it together for a long time—the prospects for the sake of eternity are staggering. In a day where many ministers and leaders are changing jobs with the next best offer, it was such a privilege to have the opportunity to do ministry with people who wanted to stay together. We grew to love each other, and see some pretty incredible things happen for the sake of the kingdom. I don't think many people have known the kind of deep joy and camaraderie that we did.

Yet this is my hope for each of us.

I believe there are similar victorious moments and break-throughs, awaiting every team that is willing to work hard on the things we have described in these pages. These moments are worth fighting for and pursuing. It is my prayer that the Lord would grant each of us grace and strength...that wherever we are in the process, we may engage fully and dare to build a great team. For there are few things as noble, nor few things as rewarding, as investing in an enduring team that makes a difference for Jesus' sake.

APPENDICES

APPENDICES

CHEDULE FOR THREE-DAY RETREAT FOR
ROLE EXPLORATION

- **Initial Suggestions**

    ♦ Get out of town (if possible)

    ♦ Bring notebook, Bible, concordance, and as many tapes,
      CDs, and books as you dare.

    ♦ If you haven't taken a gift's assessment test, try and make
      sure you work through one before you leave

    ♦ If you have ever taken a personality profile (Myers Briggs,
      D.I.S.C. etc.) bring along the results and analysis

    ♦ Go with an expectation that God will be faithful to give you
      insight and direction

- **Day One**

LEAVE MID-AFTERNOON

PARTICIPATE IN AN ACTIVITY that helps you disengage from the nor-
mal routine:

    ♦ Take a several hour motorcycle ride—preferably on a
      Harley Davidson

    ♦ Get out on the water—swimming, boating, sailing

    ♦ Get out in nature—climb, hike, ride a bicycle

- ◆ Go to the city—watch a movie, go shopping, visit a museum
- ◆ Do something you love—play golf, see an old friend, go to a concert

DINNER (LIGHT)—Consider fasting for the next twenty-four hours

EVENING: *Get updated spiritually.*

- ◆ Do some journaling about where you are spiritually.
- ◆ Have a time of worship and personal reflection/repentance
  - — Worship in a way that fits you
  - — Deal with any unresolved sin
- ◆ Listen to an inspiring tape/video on life purpose and/or releasing the laity into ministry
- ◆ Close with an extended prayer time dedicating the retreat to God's purposes

GET A GOOD NIGHT'S REST

■ *Day Two*

BEGIN DAY WITH A BRISK WALK, or some other form of light exercise

MORNING: *Make Observations*

- ◆ Look up passages from the Bible on God's purposes, spiritual gifts, and the body of Christ (use concordance if necessary)
- ◆ Listen to a tape (read book/articles) on spiritual gifts and review personality and spiritual gifts profile, and corresponding analysis. Note any observations that seem pertinent
- ◆ Take time to chronicle significant life experiences:
  - — when and where did you feel most effective
  - — when and where have you felt most affirmed

— what are the things you really love to do

— what positive intuitions about your life have stayed with you

— what you might consider to be God's word(s) to you

◆ Note any consistent themes

BREAK (LUNCH)

REST / WALK

AFTERNOON: *Ask questions*

In light of what you observed in the scriptures and about yourself (this morning), answer the following questions:

- *If you could do anything you wanted to do, and be guaranteed success what would you do?*

- *What is it about the first half of your life that sets you up for the next half?*

- *What are the most significant lessons you have learned from your failures and how might that apply to your future?*

- *What opportunities are available to you right now that might provide you the best chance to dream and achieve?*

NOTE: These can be very difficult questions to process. You could easily get stuck on any one of them. Feel free to stop, take a break, and do something different. Listen to music. Sometimes it can help to change environments, work outside, call up a friend / spouse, speak your thoughts into a tape recorder, or pray out-loud. Take lots of notes—you can sort later.

DINNER (a light one, if you have been fasting)

EVENING: *Process with someone who knows you*

Depending on your relational make-up you may want to write some summary thoughts first. Otherwise, call or visit with a friend who knows you well. Begin to share about the two or three common themes. Ask for feedback. Walk through various ideas and possibilities. Be alert to the sensation of confirmation in your soul (that which resonates with something deep inside).

RECORD YOUR CONCLUSIONS.

■ *Day Three*

SLEEP IN

GO OUT FOR BREAKFAST!

MORNING: *Commit to next steps*

PULL OUT YOUR CALENDAR and make a list of things to do:

+ Who do I need to call?

+ What do I need to do?

+ Is there anyone else I need to consult?

+ Are there other resources I need in order to proceed?

+ Do I need another retreat to clarify my conclusions?

+ What do I know now that I didn't know before?

NOTE: For our staff members it seemed to take an average of two (some times three) retreats over a 6–9 month period to gain some real confidence on these things. Don't feel discouraged if you go home with unanswered questions. It is often the combination of reflection and experimentation that clarifies the purpose-oriented issues.

RETURN HOME, AND DO WHAT YOU KNOW.

ROLE DESCRIPTIONS

EXECUTIVE PASTOR

■ *Resourcing (60%)*

I love resourcing myself, the Senior Pastor, the staff, the Board, and the congregation for the purpose of implementing the vision God has given this church. Good thinking coupled with good theology translates into effective and productive ministry. I see my role as one who "tweaks" and leads based on good research and wise counsel.

Scheduling Implications

Spend time reading, networking and studying

Give leadership for the planning, organizing, implementation, and evaluation of the ministry goals and measurement tools

Lead biweekly Management Team meetings

Help create and communicate matters for Board action

Work with Administrator on personnel policies, budgeting process, facility issues and other pertinent administrative matters

Teaching responsibilities include:

LEADERSHIP SUMMIT: annual leadership event

LEADERSHIP WOODCREST: quarterly class

LEADERSHIP HOUR: monthly luncheon

SUBSTITUTE FOR SENIOR PASTOR: 3 Sundays/year

■ *Pastoring (20%)*

I love seeing the "felt needs" of people being met. A significant part of my role in this church involves my exercising my wisdom and exhortation gifts in times of crisis. I particularly love doing this as an evangelism/assimilation tool for new attendees. I will help individuals process their dreams, concerns and hurts, and seek to get them the resources they need for spiritual, relational and emotional healing.

Scheduling Implications

> Staff Contact for Recovery Group leaders
>
> Available to congregation for counseling (by appointment)
>
> Informal but purposeful pastoral interaction with congregation on Sunday AM and at Community Live!
>
> Available for Weddings, Premarital Counseling, and Funerals
>
> Strategic shepherding and mentoring of staff and key lay leaders

■ *Assisting (10%)*

I love seeing Pieter fulfill his goals, grow in his gifts, and live in the fullness of his calling. Freeing him up to maximize his leadership and teaching gifts is my primary purpose for assuming the role of Executive Pastor. Protecting him (his time and his decisions) is a value I hold dear. Three commitments I will fulfill:

1. I won't forget that he's the boss
2. I will offer solutions when venting frustrations
3. I will not demand without an offer of resignation

Scheduling Implications

> Available to process "big picture" challenges
>
> Member of Pastoral Advisory Team
>
> "Pinch hit" in meetings and services as needed
>
> Whatever else . . .

■ **Relating (10%)**

I love "tithing" a portion of my time and ministry to the health of the larger community outside the walls of Woodcrest—both church and secular

Scheduling Implications

> Chamber of Commerce
>
> Discipleship of Community Leaders
>
> Community-wide pastor fellowships
>
> Mentoring other like-minded churches in the state
>
> Neighborhood evangelism

Administrative Pastor

■ *Building Teams and Shepherding Staff (35%)*

I love putting the right people together, at the right place and time, to create a ministry impact far greater than the individuals could do by themselves. I love to see people working together, creating ministry, taking ownership, and having fun, all striving to fulfill their part of the organizational mission.

I also desire to help people move to the next level personally and spiritually—to learn God's truth and apply it to their lives. I desire to spend one-on-one time with staff helping them with emotional, financial, spiritual, and relational struggles, so that they will be healthy and able to make a greater impact in their ministry area.

Scheduling Implications

Maintain one-on-one accountable relationships with 2–3 carefully chosen staff and lay leaders

Be available to resource staff on an as-needed basis, with personal and professional issues

Create the agenda for staff meetings

Plan staff parties, events and retreats

Resource and develop the staff Administration Team; lead team meetings

Assist Admin. staff in developing their task teams

Resource and develop the Financial Advisory Board; lead meetings

Create teams to take on special projects (database development, building, etc.)

Serve as a member of Management Team & Leadership Team

■ *Assisting the Executive Pastor (20%)*

I feel called to assist the Executive Pastor in the implementation of the vision—to use my gifts and abilities to make his God-given dreams a reality. I feel called to think in terms of strategy and purpose, making sure the organization is aligned and organized to meet its Vision 2000 goals (and beyond). I desire to help them get the job done, through the people God has called along side us.

Scheduling Implications

Consult with Rod and Pieter on areas of strategic concern

Assist with effectiveness and follow-up of Board meetings

Coach team leaders and staff on ways to increase effectiveness in reaching their goals

Coach team leaders on the effectiveness of their team structure and their staff's job responsibilities

Be looking for ways to better align all areas of the church to its mission

Assist Rod in the planning and evaluation of goals, and tying those goals to the budget process. Lead Management Team in all discussions that deal with mission implementation.

Assure that we continually engage in a strategic planning process

Assure that all goals are measured using our data tracking system

Stay connected with the heartbeat of the ministry by participating in Sunday morning, Community Live, Open House, leadership events, and other church functions.

■ *Oversee Corporate Communications (10%)*

I feel God has gifted me as a communicator. He has given me the ability to organize and synthesize information, to determine what needs to be communicated to whom, in what way, and in what time. I have a desire to use these skills in communicating important corporate issues to the staff and core, both verbally and in writing.

Scheduling Implications

> Consult with Pieter on strategies for communicating important church issues. Act as a final gate before information is communicated publicly

> Consult with Jody and R & D Team on what issues need to be covered in church publications

> Hold the value of communication for Community Live. Determine what issues should be addressed in Community Concerns, and sit on the CL Programming Team to hold that value

> Capture strategic plans and ministry philosophies on paper for future reference (position papers, etc.). Eventually compile a ministry handbook with this information.

> Verbally communicate church issues to staff, Board and lay leaders when appropriate

■ *Administrating (35%)*

I have the desire to champion the values of efficiency and effectiveness at Woodcrest, as well as champion the goal of expanding our financial base—both wider and deeper. I have the desire to use my administrative and leadership gifts to oversee the policies, procedures and personnel issues of this church, as well oversee the facility and finances.

Scheduling Implications

> Act as liaison between Administrative Team and leadership on budget & administrative issues

Act as liaison between staff and Board on administrative issues

Oversee personnel administration and development

Handle new staff orientations

Produce "Team Manual" for new staff

Further develop our compensation plan

Deal with staff conflict and discipline issues when needed

Problem solve with Administrative Team on improving facility, finance, and office operations

Educate myself on administrative issues to assure compliance in all areas

Attend NACBA conferences and work on certification

Network with other church administrators

Work on projects on an as-needed basis

Increase stewardship awareness, primarily through work with Financial Advisory Board

Work on bringing back the financial counseling ministry

Programming Director and Music Associate

- **Staying Strong (15%)**

I love for my ministry to be an authentic outgrowth of my personal walk with Christ. As a result, I will ensure that I am constantly growing as a person, that my personal relationships are relationships of integrity, and that my commitments to my wife and family are appropriately prioritized.

Scheduling Implications

> I will protect my time with my wife in order to fulfill my commitment to her, to love her as Christ loved the church. I will pursue health spiritually, emotionally, and physically in order to become the husband that God would have me to be for her.
>
> I will use one morning/week as a time for sharpening myself through worship and study.
>
> I will attend weekly staff chapel as a means of personal replenishment
>
> I will take retreats and vacations as needed/permitted/ required for rest and renewal.

- **Communicating (10%)**

I love assisting the Senior Pastor and the programming team in communicating God's truth in a culturally relevant way.

Scheduling Implications

> Lead and facilitate weekly Service Planning Meetings
>
> Provide the Sr. Pastor (or teaching pastor) with input and feedback on weekly messages

- *Creating (35%)*

I love facilitating the process by which those who are spiritually curious open their eyes and hearts to who God is and what he wants to do—not just in terms of eternity but as it relates to our daily life here on earth.

Scheduling Implications

> I will use music (my primary talent and area of expertise) as well as any other area of the arts to communicate Biblical truth with creativity and impact.

> I will chart songs as necessary for the preparation of music for our services

> I will plan and lead weekly programming meetings

> I will lead and mentor volunteer teams to help create appropriate seeker-oriented environments

- *Developing (30%)*

I love helping believers become congruent about matters of faith and practice. I want to help create environments where Christians can be challenged to live fully devoted lives such that their behaviors and relationships reflect their profession of faith.

Scheduling Implications

> I will coordinate the worship portion of Community Live!

> I will find, write, and/or produce music that provides the appropriate personal expression of praise for our worship environments

> I will build and manage volunteer teams to accomplish these goals

■ *Defining (10%)*

I love doing what we do with excellence.

Scheduling Implications

> I will uphold the value of excellence in the programming and execution of our weekly events. I do not want to place any unnecessary hindrances before people as they investigate the claims of Christ. I will attempt to model, teach, and train those within my sphere of influence to value and pursue excellence in all they do, as their own expression of worship to a worthy God.

> I will select team members and lead rehearsals in a way that allows us to accomplish this goal.